THE NEW WINDMILL SERIES

General Editors: Anne and Ian Serraillier

171

ATHENS AT WAR

This shortened version of the Greek historian
Thucydides' great book is beautifully judged, lucidly
expressed, and makes compelling reading for today.
Not only is the viewpoint balanced and very humane,
but the basic themes—of courage and nobility,
senseless brutality and betrayal of ideals—belong to
all great wars that have ever happened.

ATHENS AT WAR

retold by
REX WARNER

from 'The History of the
Peloponnesian War'
of Thucydides

Decorations by
WILLIAM STOBBS

HEINEMANN EDUCATIONAL BOOKS
LONDON

Heinemann Educational Books Ltd

LONDON   EDINBURGH   MELBOURNE   AUCKLAND   TORONTO
SINGAPORE   HONG KONG   KUALA LUMPUR
IBADAN   NAIROBI   JOHANNESBURG
NEW DELHI

ISBN 0 435 12171 5

Published by
Heinemann Educational Books Ltd
48 Charles Street, London W1X 8AH

Printed and bound in Great Britain by
Morrison and Gibb Ltd, London and Edinburgh

Contents

Foreword

THERE are many people who regard Thucydides as the greatest historian who has ever lived. He is not the easiest or the simplest. Like most historians, he gives us the facts of what happened and also an explanation for them; but he goes further than this. He makes us feel that the accurate and deeply-felt picture which he gives us is the picture not only of the war between Athens and Sparta, in which he took part, but the picture of all wars, of mankind itself. His aims are far beyond those of the war correspondent, the patriot or the entertainer. He is a humane scientist and, as he tells us himself, he is writing a work which will always be appropriate, 'human nature being what it is', and is 'a possession for ever'.

Much of the following narrative is in Thucydides' own words, taken from my translation of *The Peloponnesian War* published in the Penguin Classics, but I have shortened his story a great deal and have put in a certain amount of explanatory material where it seemed necessary. But I have made no attempt to simplify him. You cannot simplify him without destroying him, and a Thucydides adapted for reading by the very young would not be Thucydides at all.

He is above all a serious writer, and he owns himself that some readers may be put off by what he admits is the absence of 'a romantic element' in his writing. Those who know him will agree that this absence is amply made up for by his deep humanity, his scrupulous regard for truth and his bold and brilliant investigation of the causes of things.

He tells us little about himself and nothing that is not relevant to his story. For instance, that he was a young man at the outbreak of the war and lived to see its end, that he caught the plague and recovered, that he was exiled after the capture of Amphipolis and therefore, while in exile, had a good opportunity of watching events from the enemy side. All this amounts to little more than giving us his credentials. And there is much more that we would like him to have told us; for instance, how well did he know Pericles, Nicias, Alcibiades, Brasidas and others? In all probability he did know these people, and certainly a modern historian who was acquainted with, say, Churchill, Lenin, Roosevelt, Kennedy and Chairman Mao, would tell us so and probably describe his meetings with them. But to Thucydides, as to most classical writers, these personal revelations seem to be beside the point. As there is no 'romantic element', so there is no gossip, much as we might like to hear it.

He is often called 'impersonal', 'objective' and 'scientific', and rightly so. But if these adjectives give us the idea of anything like a mechanical computer or of a scientist who is not passionately and emotionally involved in his work, they will conceal the truth from us. The same adjectives could be used of the great tragic poets of Thucydides' time, Sophocles and Euripides, and they would refer to a precision of style and thought, not to any lack of feeling.

So a reader of Thucydides should be able to see that the precision and force of his style are not the result of a suppression of emotion, but are its fitting expression. He, just as much as the dramatists, felt pity and terror to the full. He had also, as they had in different ways, a profound sense of patriotism.

It seems evident that from his youth he was passionately committed to the ideal of Pericles. And, as the years passed, he saw with anguish how this ideal was, under the storm of war and danger, utterly degraded. The practical idealism of Pericles is replaced by the vulgar cynicism of Cleon or the more subtle and even more shocking cynicism of the Athenian ambassadors at Melos. Cleon, it is true, sometimes uses phrases which might have been used by Pericles, but the meaning has utterly changed. Indeed one of Thucydides' most important lessons to us today is that in revolutionary times, as he notes in the sombre description of the revolution in Corcyra, words do change their meanings.

In some passages it will appear that he mistrusts and is appalled by what he calls 'human nature', which, where circumstances cause the collapse of the restraints of religion, law and a decent convention, quickly reverts to brutality and savagery. But alongside these passages we should set his abiding faith in the Athens of which Pericles had dreamed and which, for a short time, actually existed. His experience had shown him that 'human nature' was capable of rising to the greatest heights as well as sinking to the lowest depths. And here his vision may be compared with that of Sophocles.

Like Sophocles and Euripides too, he feels intensely for those who, for no fault of their own, become involved in misery or suffering for which there seems no justification. Examples of this can be found in his account of the massacre of the school children by Thracian barbarians in the little town of Mycalessus—an event which made no difference at all to the course of the war—and, in particular, in his treatment of Nicias in the last days of the Sicilian expedition.

His theme is politics in the very widest sense and his work is, I believe, the best work on politics that has ever been written. But its greatness depends not only on the strict and sincere analysis of cause and effect but on depth of feeling and what may be described as the consolation of the tragic faith—that, in spite of appearances so miserably to the contrary, man is heroic and justice exists.

REX WARNER

Introduction

AT the outbreak of the great war between Athens and
Sparta, I, Thucydides, a citizen of Athens, was a young
man. The war lasted nearly thirty years and I have lived to
see the end of it.

I started the writing of my history at the very beginning
of the war and I did this because I believed that it was going
to be the most important war that had ever been fought and
the one most worth writing about. Not everyone at the time
would have accepted this view. People are apt to glorify the
past and to give it more value than it really has. All Greeks,
for instance, are familiar with Homer and Homer has written
so well of the ancient Greek expedition against Troy that we
are inclined to think that it was on a much greater scale than

could possibly have been the case. In fact the numbers involved were not large, the tactics employed were primitive and the result achieved was inconsiderable. And after the Trojan War what order there had been in Greece broke down. Poets and storytellers tend to disguise the fact that civilisation as we know it is a very recent thing.

A far greater war than the Trojan War was that fought by the Persians against Greece and which some of the older men of my time can remember. In this war large armies and navies took part and difficult problems of supply were adequately dealt with. Yet in this war the decision was reached quickly as the result of only two naval battles and two battles on land.

But the war between Athens and Sparta not only lasted a long time, but caused more suffering to the Greeks than any other war. Never before had so many cities been captured and then devastated; never had so many people been killed in battle, in revolution, by plague and famine or in cold blood. At the beginning both Athens and Sparta were at the height of their power, and every other state in Greece was ranged on one side or the other. Persia too intervened before the war ended, so that not only the whole of Greece, but, one may almost say, the whole known world was involved.

My method in writing this history differs from that of the poets, who exaggerate the importance of their themes, and from that of most writers in prose, whose chief aim is to make themselves agreeable to their readers. My aim has been to find out the truth of what really happened and, so far as possible, the reasons why things happened in this way. In the actions and debates which I have described I was either present myself or else have relied upon the reports of others who were present, and I have checked these reports with as much thoroughness as I could. Even so the truth was not always easy to find out. Different eyewitnesses will give different accounts of the same events, either out of bias for one side or the other or because of imperfect memories. In order to make clear the action and to define the reasons behind it I have made use of set speeches which were delivered either before or during the war. To many of these I listened myself, but have found it difficult to remember the precise words that were used. So, while keeping as closely as I could to the sense of what was actually said, I have allowed the speakers to use what, in my opinion, were the words called for by each situation.

In the second part of the war I was living in exile and so I have been able to collect evidence from both sides and have therefore, perhaps, been able to gain a clearer insight into the minds of my country's enemies than if I had been all the time in Athens.

I must own that there is nothing romantic or picturesque about my history and this may be a disappointment to some readers. But I shall be content if in future times my words are found useful by those people who want to understand clearly the events which happened in the past and which (human nature being what it is) will, at some time or other and in much the same ways, be repeated in the future. My book was not written to catch the taste of the moment. It was written to last for ever.

1. The Background

WHEN war broke out between Athens and Sparta, each side could complain with some reason that it was the other side which was responsible. But the events which immediately led to the war were not the real cause of the war. What made it inevitable was the growth of Athenian power and the fear which this caused in Sparta.

At the time of the Persian invasions, some fifty or sixty years before this war, Sparta had been unquestionably the leading power in Greece. All this had changed, and had changed with extraordinary rapidity. Athens was now recognised to be at least as strong as Sparta; indeed many would say that she was already far stronger. And what particularly alarmed the Spartans was that the power of

Athens rested on methods, tactics, politics and a whole way of life which was unlike anything that had ever been known or imagined in Sparta.

There had been two Persian invasions of Greece, separated from each other by about ten years. The first invasion was directed primarily against Athens and one of the Great King's aims in sending out an expeditionary force was to restore to power in Athens the family of the Athenian Peisistratus which had ruled as dictators before Athens adopted the new system of government known as democracy. The invasion, of course, threatened not only Athens but the whole of Greece, and the Athenian democracy had appealed to Sparta for help. As so often in her history, Sparta and her allies moved slowly and, it would seem, reluctantly. The Persian army landed on the coast of Attica and was there defeated at Marathon by the Athenians alone, aided by a contingent from their ally, the small city of Plataea. When the battle was over the Spartan army arrived, visited the battlefield and marched home again.

At this time the Persian empire extended from India to the shores of Greece. Egypt was already part of it. The Greek cities of Asia Minor, the Black Sea and the Aegean islands were under Persian domination. It seemed to be something incredible that this world power should have suffered a defeat at the hands of one Greek city and that not the strongest. Marathon is a name that the Athenians have never forgotten.

But the plans of the Persians were not seriously disturbed by this set-back. Ten years later Xerxes, the Great King, in person led a far more formidable army into Greece and this time it was supported by an enormous fleet, numerically much stronger than the combined naval forces of the Greeks. According to the historian Herodotus, the Persian host numbered five million and they drank rivers dry on their march. The number is exaggerated, but there may well have been half a million on the march; as for the drinking dry of rivers, this would depend, I imagine, on how much water was in the rivers at the time the army came to them. For parts of the year many rivers in Greece are dry anyway. It is certain, however, that this huge force was adequately supplied and that, when it reached the plains of northern Greece, it was in good order and, to all appearance, invincible.

The supreme command in the defence of Greece was, as was traditional, in the hands of Sparta who, with her allies, could certainly put the largest army into the field. A Spartan admiral was also in command of the Greek fleet, although much the greatest contingent in the fleet came from Athens.

The first attempt to resist the Persian invasion was made at the pass of Thermopylae where an advance guard of not more than six thousand men, after a very gallant resistance under the command of the Spartan king Leonidas, was overwhelmed and virtually destroyed. At the same time the Greek navy had attempted to hold back the Persian fleet in the channel between Euboea and the mainland. Here the Persians lost many ships in a storm and in the subsequent naval battle at Artemisium they did little better than hold their own. But the Greek defeat at Thermopylae made it necessary for the fleet also to retire. The whole of northern Greece was now open to the Persians, who occupied Thebes and then marched unopposed to Athens, burning the Greek

cities on their way.

Athens was now the only state in northern Greece which had not gone over to Persia. The city itself was unprotected, since the allied army had withdrawn behind the Isthmus of Corinth, across which they were building a defensive wall. This wall, of course, would be valueless if the Persians gained command of the sea, a thing which would certainly have happened if the Athenian fleet had gone over to the enemy.

At this time the most influential Athenian statesman and the most intelligent and brilliant commander among the Greeks was Themistocles. He had played a great part in the building of the Athenian navy and he seems to have seen more clearly than anyone else that the future of Athens was to depend on sea power. The later Athenian statesman Pericles, who was only a boy at this time, shared and was to develop many of Themistocles' ideas.

Now Themistocles persuaded his countrymen to take to their ships, and to leave behind their city, their property and the temples of their gods. Non-combatants and what property could be moved were evacuated to Salamis and other nearby islands. The able-bodied manned the ships as sailors or as marines. The few who had refused to leave the city were massacred by the Persians, and soon the Athenians on Salamis could see the sky black with smoke from the burning of the Acropolis, of the temples and of their houses.

In later times the Athenians would claim that no other state had made such sacrifices for the cause of Greek freedom and that no other state had made such an important contribution to the final victory. There is much to justify

such a claim. The most telling success of the war was the Greek naval victory at Salamis, a victory won by the tactics of Themistocles and, very largely, by the courage and skill of the large Athenian contingent of ships. King Xerxes, sitting on a golden throne overlooking the bay of Salamis, had seen the destruction of his fleet. With a large part of his army, much of which was lost on the way, he returned to Persia, leaving behind in northern Greece a force which was still formidable under his commander Mardonius.

Next year Mardonius moved southward from his bases in Thessaly. Again the Spartans and their allies were slow in marching north and again Attica was devastated by the Persians. Finally, however, the combined Greek army, under the Spartan Pausanias, defeated the Persians in the plain of Plataea, not far north of Athens. On the same day the Greek navy won another decisive victory at Mycale on the coast of Asia Minor. Though there were still Persian troops in Europe, the immediate danger to mainland Greece was over.

Up to this time, in spite of many differences, the Spartans and Athenians had worked well together. At Plataea the Spartan infantry had fully lived up to its great reputation. But the Athenians too had fought well at Plataea and had put into the field the second largest army on the Greek side. And on the sea Athens was undoubtedly the strongest power in Greece. The history of the next fifty years is the history of growing divergence and opposition between Athens and Sparta, sometimes in peace and sometimes in war, until the great war between the two states and their allies broke out.

The obvious differences between Athens and Sparta were these: Sparta was a land power with a tightly organised government in which power was in the hands of a few men; the Spartans were a minority of highly trained soldiers living in a territory that was largely populated by subject peoples, known as 'helots', and always fearing that these helots might revolt; on the whole the Spartans were content to hold their dominant position in the Peloponnese, where among their allies they favoured the system of oligarchy, or government by a few; they distrusted innovation in politics, in art and in ideas. Athens, on the other hand, was a sea power and a democracy; far from being content with their own country of Attica, the Athenians were always going further and further afield; they were intensely proud of their form of government and they tended to support democracies in other states; they were always innovators; they welcomed new ideas and were already beginning to produce an art and literature unique in history.

Now that the immediate threat to mainland Greece was no longer felt, the Spartans were content to go back to the state of affairs that had existed beforehand. They had little or no interest in liberating the Greeks of Asia Minor and the islands which had for some time been under the Persians. They did not like foreign adventures and their intensely conservative government had noticed that Spartan officers, once they started living abroad, were apt to become arrogant, undisciplined and, to their minds, un-Spartan.

The attitude of the Athenians was just the opposite. They had won great victories and they were eager to follow them up. Also most of the Greek colonists overseas in the islands

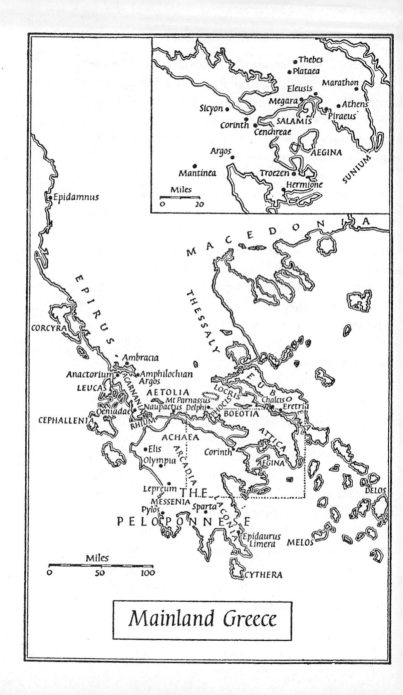

Mainland Greece

and on the Asiatic coast were Ionians, speaking a Greek that was very like that of Attica and with a long tradition which they shared with Athens. They had lived in Greece long before the invasions or infiltrations of Dorians, among whom Sparta was the leading state, and they naturally looked to Athens as their ally and protector on the mainland.

Directly after the victories of Plataea and Mycale the Athenians began rebuilding the fortifications of their city which had been destroyed by the Persians. The Spartans objected. According to them it would be better for there to be no fortifications in any city in northern Greece, and they invited the Athenians to join with them in insisting that all existing fortifications should be destroyed. This, they said, would make it impossible for the Persians in any future invasion to secure a strong base, as they had at Thebes.

Whether or not this suggestion was put forward in good faith by the Spartans, it was wholly unacceptable to the Athenians. They had already seen their city destroyed and had no intention of remaining quiet until the Persians were strong enough to invade again. Also the effect of carrying out the Spartan plan would be that, since Sparta could muster the largest army in Greece, no Greek state would be able to act independently of Sparta. And the Athenians were determined to be independent.

What they did was to send Themistocles to Sparta where he engaged the Spartans in prolonged discussions about their proposals. Meanwhile in Athens men, women and children hurried on with the work of fortifying the city. Even today you can see in the walls of the Athenian Acropolis how they used every piece of building material available

—the drums of temple columns, unshaped stone, fragments of sculpture, anything that would serve the purpose. So at one point in the still unfinished discussion at Sparta Themistocles was able to announce that further debate was unnecessary, since the walls were already completed.

Themistocles also persuaded the Athenians to finish fortifying their system of harbours at Piraeus. He saw that the future of Athens was to be based on sea power and if one can say that any one man was the founder of the Athenian empire, that man was Themistocles.

Athens had now shown her independence and the Spartans had to accept the position with what grace they could. But they never forgave Themistocles.

The next shift in the balance of power was provoked by the Spartans themselves. After his victory at Plataea, the Spartan Pausanias took over the command of the Greek fleet operating in the northern Aegean. Much the greater part of the fleet came from Athens and from the large Aegean islands of Chios, Lesbos and Samos. This fleet won important victories during the year, ending with the liberation of Byzantium from the Persians, but Pausanias behaved in so arrogant and dictatorial a way that he made himself insupportable to the rest of the allies.

The commander of the Athenian contingent at the time was Aristides. He had distinguished himself at the battle of Salamis and had a great reputation for integrity. The leaders of the allies now approached him, telling him that they were unwilling to serve any longer under Pausanias and asking the Athenians to take over the command. At about the same time Pausanias was called home by the Spartan government.

He was suspected, among other things, of intriguing with the Persians and was later put to death. By the time a new commander had been sent out from Sparta, it was found that the allies had all committed themselves to Athenian leadership. The Spartans were quite content to leave things as they found them. They had no wish to continue the war and no great experience in naval warfare or in the kind of combined operations which would be necessary. They believed Athens to be perfectly friendly to them and saw in her no serious threat to their own position as leader of the Greeks.

In this way was formed the Athenian League, later to be called an Empire. It was originally a voluntary league of independent states, among whom Athens was recognised as the leader. The headquarters of the League was in the island of Delos and representative meetings were held in the temple there. Fixed contributions were laid down for each state; some provided ships and men for the allied forces which were to operate against Persia; others preferred to make their contributions in money. In many cases those who preferred to make money contributions were those who were willing to let the Athenians do the fighting. The result, of course, was that the Athenian navy grew more and more powerful, while the allied states became relatively weaker and weaker. Before very long only the larger states in the alliance, such as the islands of Chios, Lesbos and Samos, had any navy at all. The Athenian leadership was extremely efficient and, as success followed success, some of the states began to feel themselves secure and to resent having to meet their obligations. The Athenians, on the other hand, were convinced that, if the alliance were to be effective, it must be tightly organised. When, four years after the foundation of the League, one state, the island of Naxos, attempted to leave the alliance, an allied force was sent against it and it was compelled to come back to its allegiance on harsher terms than before. The same thing happened later in other cases.

At the time of the revolt of Naxos the Athenian commander was Cimon. His father was Miltiades who had commanded the Athenian army at Marathon. The greatest of all Cimon's many victories took place some years later when at the river Eurymedon in southern Asia Minor he captured or destroyed a Persian fleet of two hundred ships and followed this up by a crushing defeat of a large Persian army on land. This victory gave Athens and her allies complete naval supremacy in the Aegean and along the coasts of Asia Minor. It now seemed to many of the allies that the purposes of the alliance had been achieved, but to Athens one victory was just a step to further conquest.

In politics Cimon was for carrying on the war with Persia with the utmost energy while at the same time remaining friendly and loyal to Sparta. On the latter point he differed from Themistocles who, as he had shown, was quite prepared to oppose Sparta in the interests of Athenian independence. And the Athenians, for the time being, had chosen to follow Cimon. Themistocles, in spite of the great part he had played in making Athens a sea-power and in the victory of Salamis, was first exiled and then accused by Sparta of having intrigued, like Pausanias, with the Persians. He was forced to take refuge at the Persian court, where he was treated with great honour by the Persian king. After his death, his friends secretly brought back his bones and buried them in Athenian soil. No one knows where they lie.

In spite of Cimon's efforts, the friendly co-operation between Athens and Sparta was not to last for long. In Athens younger statesmen, among whom the most important was Pericles, followed and enlarged the policies of Themistocles. They aimed at a more thorough-going democracy and at a still greater extension of Athenian sea power, and they objected strongly to any interference with Athenian affairs by the Spartans. And the policy of Sparta herself played into their hands. First it became known in Athens that the Spartans had offered help to one of the Athenian allies which had revolted from the alliance. The help was never given and the ally, the island of Thasos, was forced to surrender and accept Athenian terms. But this incident strengthened the anti-Spartan party in Athens.

Soon after the capitulation of Thasos Cimon was able to persuade his countrymen to do one more favour to Sparta, but this was the last. An earthquake had done immense damage in Sparta herself and at the same time the subject population was in revolt. The Spartans made a desperate appeal to Athens for help and Cimon came to their aid with a large Athenian army. This help arrived just in time and may even have saved Sparta from extinction. But the Spartans were far from showing gratitude. From the first they distrusted the Athenians, whose manners and whole way of life were so unlike their own. They saw in them a kind of revolutionary spirit of which they were greatly afraid and they began to fear that these men might end up by sympathising with the rebels. So, after the immediate danger was over, they asked the Athenians, alone of their allies, to go away again.

To the army and to the people at home this action of the Spartans seemed an intolerable insult and they blamed Cimon for having made it possible. Soon afterwards, he was exiled and though, some years later, he was recalled and once more led an army and a fleet to victory, he was never again in control of Athenian policy. For the next thirty years by far the most influential statesman was Pericles.

It was a period of enormous Athenian expansion in every direction. Athenian armies and navies fought in central Greece, round the coasts of the Peloponnese and Asia, in Egypt and on the islands. There were victories and there were set-backs, but at the end of the period Athens was stronger than she had ever been. For a time she had controlled not only the seas but also large areas of the mainland. This empire in central Greece and the northern Peloponnese she was forced to give up, but as a result she became still stronger on the sea and her empire in the islands and on the Aegean coastline became larger and more firmly organised. After some thirty years of fighting a peace with Persia had been made. All the aims of the original League had been carried out, but there was now no question of allowing any of the originally independent member states to leave the confederacy. The Treasury of the League had now been moved from Delos to Athens. The money spent, as before, in strengthening the Athenian navy, but it was also spent on a tremendous building programme designed for the beautification and greater glory of Athens.

The conservative opponents of Pericles criticised him for spending the money of the allies on magnificent buildings and on splendid exhibitions of Athenian drama, art and poetry. Some even ventured to declare that, since the war with Persia was over, Athens had accomplished her task and the allies should be left free to go their own ways.

But Pericles believed that the empire was necessary for the very survival of Athens. He also believed, with reason, that Athens was the most enlightened state in Greece, a model to all other states, and, since power had to be exercised by someone, the state best adapted to exercise its power fairly and generously. Athens, to his mind, gave much more than she received. And she was now perfectly secure. The famous Long Walls had been built from Athens to the harbour of Piraeus and, so long as Athens retained the command of the sea, she was impregnable to any attack.

For some fourteen years before the outbreak of the great war between Athens and Sparta there had been peace, but little collaboration, between the two states. The peace treaty, which was officially meant to last for thirty years, was a recognition of the equality of the two systems of alliances. Sparta had recovered her strength after the dangers of the war with her subjects. Her infantry was still regarded as the strongest in the world. But Sparta remained, as she always had been, somewhat shut in on herself and quite content to be so. Athens, on the other hand, was continually going further, continually growing. She did not interfere with Sparta, but, with her hands free in the east, she was now pushing out westwards. Her navies visited the Greek cities of Italy and Sicily, possibly with designs to bring this part of the Greek world also into the Athenian alliance.

It was a situation which might, and did, arouse fear in Sparta.

2. Sparta Decides on War

IT was in the thirteenth year of the Thirty Years' Peace made between Athens and Sparta when a meeting of her allies was called at Sparta to decide whether or not war should be declared against Athens. The state in the Spartan alliance which was most urgent for war was Corinth. She had once been the most considerable naval power in Greece, with fleets operating both in the Aegean and in the west and, from her position on the Isthmus, she was excellently placed in this respect. She was still the most important, indeed almost the only, naval power in the Spartan alliance, but she had fallen far behind Athens. Naturally she was jealous of Athenian supremacy on the sea and she now had, or thought she had, two grievances against Athens.

The first of these concerned an alliance which had recently been made between Athens and the large island of Corcyra off the west coast of Greece. Corcyra was originally a colony of Corinth, but was now an independent state with a considerable navy of her own. At the time of the Thirty Years' Peace she was not a member of either the Spartan or the Athenian alliance, but, finding herself threatened by Corinth, she had recently applied to join the Athenian alliance, pointing out that her large fleet would greatly strengthen Athens, whereas, if she were subdued by Corinth, and forced into the Spartan alliance, the enemies of Athens would be greatly strengthened on the sea. The Athenians saw the force of this argument. Also there was nothing legally wrong with the wish of Corcyra to join them, since Corcyra had been neutral at the time of the peace treaty. At the same time it would be a breach of the treaty if Athens were to join Corcyra in any aggression against Sparta's ally, Corinth. The Athenians therefore concluded a defensive alliance with Corcyra.

Soon after this the Corinthians with a fleet of one hundred and fifty ships sailed against Corcyra. The Athenians sent out a token force of ten ships, with orders not to engage in any actual fighting unless the Corinthians attempted to land on Corcyraean territory. The Athenians so far obeyed their orders that in the naval battle which took place they put their ten ships into line of battle with the one hundred and ten ships of Corcyra, but, although they made a show of fighting, they did not sink an enemy ship until the Corinthian fleet had been victorious and were forcing the Corcyraeans, with great loss, back to shore.

After their victory the Corinthian ships sailed in and out of the sinking or disabled enemy ships and massacred the crews. They then prepared for another assault on the remainder of the Corcyraean fleet and the ten Athenian ships. The Corcyraeans had lost about seventy ships, but again prepared for action. But just as, late in the day, the two sides were on the point of engaging, the Corinthians suddenly backed water and retired. The reason was that they had seen in the distance twenty more Athenian ships approaching. These had been sent out after the original ten, since the Athenians thought (rightly, as it turned out) that the ten would not be enough to influence the action. Now the mere sight of an Athenian fleet, small as it was, was sufficient to check the Corinthians, who had already been victorious and were still in greatly superior numbers. So great was the prestige of the Athenian navy at this time.

Next day the Corinthians accused Athens of having made war on her contrary to the terms of the Thirty Years' Peace treaty. The Athenians replied that they were not making war; they were simply protecting the territory of their ally Corcyra.

A more serious confrontation between Athens and Corinth occurred almost immediately afterwards. This concerned the important strategic town of Potidaea in the northern Aegean. This city was a colony of Corinth, with whom she had strong ties, and also a member of the Athenian alliance, paying a yearly contribution in money. Potidaea now revolted from Athens and the Corinthians sent an army of their own into the town. In this case the Corinthians could claim provocation, but their action was unquestionably in violation of the existing treaty. Athens lost no time in sending out a strong force to besiege Potidaea and soon blockaded the place with the Corinthians inside.

So far there had been fighting only between Athens and Corinth. Sparta, however much she sympathised with Corinth and secretly encouraged her, had kept the peace. Now took place the debate at Sparta in which the Corinthians in particular urged Sparta into war. They were supported by Megara, a city lying between Corinth and Athens. Megara had once been forced into the Athenian alliance, but, by the terms of the peace treaty, had reverted to her alliance with Sparta. Later she had sent ships to aid Corinth against Corcyra and the Athenians had passed a decree excluding her from all the ports in their alliance. Since Megara depended largely on foreign trade, this was a very damaging blow to her economy.

There was already at Sparta a strong feeling that war was inevitable and that, since Athens was growing stronger every day, the sooner it came, the better. But there were also others who could foresee the risks involved and were reluctant to move until they were better prepared, particularly on the sea.

The delegates from Corinth insisted that now or never was the time for putting an end to what they called Athenian aggression and they blamed the Spartans for not already having acted. In the course of their speech they said:

'Athens has already deprived many Greek states of their freedom and, as is shown by what has happened at Corcyra and at Potidaea, is planning the enslavement of all Greece. And it is you, Spartans, who are responsible for all this.

First you allowed the Athenians to fortify their city and build their Long Walls after the Persian War. Since then you have done nothing to prevent them going from strength to strength. No doubt you mean well, but you are naturally slow to act and slow to think. You have never even tried to imagine what sort of people these Athenians are and how utterly different they are from you. An Athenian is always the innovator, quick to make decisions and quick at carrying them out. You, on the other hand, like things to remain as they are; you are slow to come to a decision and, even when you do, you only carry it out partially. You prefer to stay at home, but the Athenians are always abroad; they think that the further they go, the more they will get, while you think that any movement you make will endanger what you have already. If you have a slight set-back, you immediately become discouraged; they, if they do suffer a defeat, will immediately follow it up by a victory. They regard their lives as expendable for the sake of their city, and at the same time each single one of them is cultivating his own intelligence, again with the idea of doing something notable for Athens. They prefer danger and action to peace and quiet. They are incapable either of living a quiet life themselves or of allowing anyone else to do so.

'We think that your whole way of life is out of date when compared with theirs. And it is just as true in politics as it is in any art or craft: new methods must drive out old ones. No doubt, if one can live in peace and quiet, the old established ways are best; but when one is constantly being faced by new problems, one has also to be capable of approaching them in an original way. And so Athens, because of the very variety of her experience, is a more modern state than you are.

'And now we call upon you at last to act. We are ready to help you. But if you wait much longer, we may be unable to do so. We have long and gladly accepted you as the leaders of the Peloponnese. It is now your duty to maintain its greatness and to liberate the rest of Greece.'

There happened to be some Athenian representatives in Sparta at this time who had come there on other business. When they heard what was going on, they asked to be allowed to speak also and the Spartans agreed to this. The Athenians had no intention of defending themselves. It seemed to them that their empire was their own affair and they were not prepared to tolerate interference by Sparta or anyone else. But they wanted to state their position clearly and, if possible, to convince the Spartans that it was in everyone's interest to keep the peace.

They began by referring to their record against the Persians—how they had stood alone against them at Marathon, how in the next invasion they had lost everything and still fought on, and how they had saved not only themselves but also Sparta and the rest of Greece at the battle of Salamis where, out of the four hundred Greek ships, more than two-thirds were Athenian. Then, after the Spartans had returned to their own country, Athens had fought the war to a finish. Her allies had formed the alliance voluntarily. No one had been forced to join. Later, certainly, it had been found necessary to keep the alliance properly organised for efficiency. Sparta would have done the same thing and in fact always had done the same thing with regard to her own alliance in the Peloponnese. And the Athenians summed up their position in these words:

'We have done nothing extraordinary, nothing contrary to human nature in accepting an empire when it was offered to us and then in refusing to give it up. Three very powerful motives prevent us from doing so—security, honour and self-interest. And we were not the first to act in this way. Far from it. It has always been a rule that the weak should be subject to the strong; and besides we consider that we are worthy of our power. You used to think that we were too, and it is only now, when you imagine yourselves to be threatened, that you have begun to talk in terms of right and wrong. Such considerations have never yet prevented a strong power from making use of its opportunities. Those who really deserve praise are the people who, while human enough to enjoy power, nevertheless pay more attention to justice than they are compelled to do. We regard ourselves as fit to exercise power and say that we exercise it more moderately than anyone else in our situation would do. We think that if you were in our position you would have made yourselves by now much more hated than we are. The fact is, as was shown during the short time that you led Greece against the Persians, that your rigid and strict way of life does not mix well with the ways of others. And indeed when you do go abroad, you do not follow either your own rules or the rules of other people.

'We advise you to think carefully before you break the peace. If you engage in war, it will be a long war, and the longer it lasts the more likely things are to depend on accidents which no one can foresee. Our treaty provides that all disputes should be submitted to arbitration. We are ready to do this and we are not going to be the first to go back on the solemn agreements we have both made. But if you decide to make war on us, we shall meet you in any and every field of action that you may choose.'

After listening to the complaints of their allies and to this Athenian reply, the Spartans asked all strangers to withdraw and began to discuss the matter among themselves. Most of them were already in favour of war, but the Spartan King Archidamus, a man who had had much experience in war and peace, made a carefully argued speech counselling moderation. He agreed that Athens was acting aggressively to Sparta's allies and that something should be done to stop her, but insisted that now was not the right time to engage in a full-scale war. He pointed out that the strength of Athens did not depend on her army. So long as she had enough men to man her fortifications, she was secure on land. Her real source of strength was in her navy and in the money she received in contributions from her allies. This strength could never be broken until Sparta and her allies could produce a fleet comparable with that of Athens. Athens could only be defeated if her allies were to revolt from her, and so long as Sparta was unable to challenge Athens on the sea, it would be impossible to bring help to any Athenian ally which did revolt. So his advice was to begin at once to build ships and train crews for them and to raise the money which would be necessary for a long war, if war should come. It was Sparta who would have to bear the brunt of the war and Sparta should not be swept away by the speeches of her allies, none of whom would put so many men into the field as herself. It was all very well for them to call her slow and cautious. But 'slow' and 'cautious' could equally well mean 'wise' and 'sensible'. And finally the Athenians were prepared to accept arbitration in accordance with the terms of the treaty. It would be wrong of Sparta not to be equally willing to abide by those terms.

After King Archidamus had spoken, the last speech of the day was made by Sthenelaidas, one of the ephors for the year. In Sparta there are five ephors or 'guardians' and these men have more power than anyone else in the state. In battle one of the two kings is in command of the army, but he is always accompanied by two ephors and can be called to account by them if there is anything amiss in his conduct. Sthenelaidas now spoke in favour of war. His speech was short and typically Spartan; for the Spartans like to think that they speak little and speak to the point.

He said: 'I do not understand these long speeches that the Athenians make. They say a lot in praise of themselves, but don't attempt to deny that they are injuring our allies. If in fact they have a fine record against the Persians and now have a bad record with regard to us, it simply means that they were once good and are now bad, and they should be made to suffer all the more for it. Also I am against this talk of arbitration. That is a question of words and lawsuits. It is not words but deeds which are injuring our allies. The Athenians may have a lot of ships and a lot of money, but we have good allies and we ought not to let them down. And so, Spartans, I call upon you to vote for the honour of Sparta and for war.'

Then the great majority of the Spartans showed that

they were in favour of war. The representatives of the allies were called in again and informed of the decision. This was ratified at a later date by a full meeting of all the states in the Spartan alliance.

In reaching their decision the Spartans were not so much influenced by the speeches of their allies as by the fact that they feared the further growth of Athenian power, seeing, as they did, that already the greater part of Greece was under the control of Athens.

3. The First Year of the War

THE Spartans were aware that once they invaded Athenian territory it would appear, whatever they might say, that it was they, not Athens, who had broken the peace treaty. There were also still some Spartans, like King Archidamus, who were against hasty action. So instead of invading at once they began by asking Athens to make various concessions. First they demanded that Athens should give up the siege of Potidaea. They also let it be understood that peace was still possible if the Athenians would cancel the decree banning the ships of Megara from her markets.

The Athenians refused to make any of these concessions and the Spartans then sent their final ultimatum. It stated simply: 'Sparta wants peace. Peace is still possible if you will give the Greeks their freedom.'

The Athenians now held an assembly to debate the whole question of peace and war. There were some who still held to the policy of Cimon, who wanted friendship with Sparta and who believed that if peace could be secured simply by revoking the Megarian decree, that was a small enough concession and one well worth making.

To these views Pericles was utterly and entirely opposed and he had been for long far the most influential speaker and the most effective man of action in Athens. He told the Athenians that Sparta, instead of settling her differences by arbitration in accordance with the treaty, was now trying to dictate terms as though she were a superior power. Under such conditions, he said, it would be unworthy of Athens to make even the very smallest concession. As for a Spartan invasion, Athens had nothing serious to fear from that. The fortifications of Athens and Piraeus were impregnable and if Sparta invaded by land, Athens was perfectly able to invade Spartan territory by sea, landing troops along the coast at any point she liked. So long as Athens controlled the seas, she was perfectly secure and the Spartans would soon grow tired of a war in which they suffered more damage than they could inflict. The strategy to be followed was this: not to risk a pitched battle against the whole force of Sparta and her allies, but to do all the damage possible to Spartan territory with sea-borne troops: to preserve the empire intact, but not to attempt to add to it while the war was in progress. If these rules were followed, an Athenian victory was certain. 'What I fear,' Pericles said, 'is not the enemy's strategy, but your own mistakes.' And he urged his fellow citizens to reply to the Spartan ambassadors that, while they were ready to reach a settlement on fair and equal terms by arbitration, they would do nothing under duress.

The Athenians voted as he asked them to do. The Spartan ambassadors returned and no further embassy was sent. Both sides prepared for war.

But before there had been any fighting between Athenians and Spartans, Sparta's ally Thebes made an unprovoked attack on the town of Plataea which lies just north of the frontier of Attica and which had long been a faithful ally of Athens. Thebes, who regarded herself as the leader of all Boeotia, had always resented the independence of Plataea and also the fine reputation Plataea had won in the Persian War; for at that time Thebes had gone over to the Persians. Now Thebes was anxious to secure an advantage before hostilities between Athens and Sparta broke out. With the help of a pro-Theban party in Plataea a force of Thebans was introduced into the town during the hours before dawn, and the Plataeans, when they woke up, found their city already occupied. At first it seemed that they would have to accept the situation and so they entered into negotiations with their enemies. But as the morning wore on they began to realise that the Theban force was not so big as they had at first thought. Since most of the Plataeans hated the Thebans and valued their alliance with Athens, they decided to resist. They thought it best to attack during the night, since, while they knew their own town, the Thebans would be confused in the darkness. And so it turned out. At a given signal the Plataeans attacked the occupying army from all directions. There was a terrific uproar. Women and slaves from the roofs hurled down tiles on the Thebans, who were taken utterly by surprise. It was a moonless night and in the darkness, which was only lit by the glare of torches, the Thebans quickly lost contact with each other. Since the situation seemed hopeless, they attempted to fight their way out, but the gates were barred and barricades were across the streets. Many of them were killed and one large body of troops rushed into a big building which formed part of the city wall. The doors of this building happened to be open and the Thebans had thought that they were gates leading outside the city. Now they found they were trapped and, fearing that the Plataeans would set fire to the building, they surrendered unconditionally.

Meanwhile a large Theban army was on the way from Thebes. They had only eight miles to go, but were delayed by heavy rain and swollen rivers. When they arrived, they found that the Plataeans had destroyed or captured the whole of the original force and they retired, hoping to get the prisoners back.

The news of the Theban attack had reached Athens and the Athenians immediately arrested all Boeotians in Attica. When they heard later that the Plataeans had defeated the invaders, they sent a message urging the Plataeans not to do anything irrevocable about the prisoners until they had consulted with Athens. But when the messenger arrived, he found that the Plataeans had already put to death all their prisoners. There were one hundred and eighty of them. Afterwards the Athenians marched to Plataea, brought food

The Aegean

and supplies into the place and left a garrison behind. They then brought back to Athens the women, the children and the men who were too old to fight.

Immediately after this affair at Plataea the army of Sparta and her allies under the command of King Archidamus marched against Attica. Before actually crossing the Athenian frontier he sent a Spartan officer to see whether at this last moment the Athenians might be willing to come to terms. But Pericles had passed a decree that no Spartan ambassador should be admitted to the city once the Spartans had marched out of the Peloponnese. So they sent Archidamus' messenger back under escort. When he reached the frontier he said: 'This day will be the beginning of great misfortunes to Greece.'

Pericles kept to his original strategy. The whole population of Attica was to withdraw behind the fortifications of Athens and Piraeus. Cattle and movable property were carried over to Euboea and other islands off shore; and a large sea-borne force was to sail round the Peloponnese, making landings wherever most damage could be done. No general engagement was to be fought with the enemy on land. This strategy, excellent as it was, entailed many hardships on those who were used to living outside the city and, for other reasons, was unpopular with many of the other citizens. People are naturally attached to their farms and property, and the Athenians who lived in the country were all the more reluctant to leave their homes since it seemed that they had only just settled into them after the devastation caused by the Persian War. A few had places to go to in Athens, but most of them had to take up cramped quarters in the city temples or in the space between the Long Walls. They were overcrowded and largely inactive and meanwhile the Peloponnesian army was burning their crops and cutting down their olive and fruit trees. It was true that, as Pericles had told them, houses could be quickly rebuilt, that, so long as Athens controlled the seas, she could import anything she wanted and that, so long as she did not risk her whole army in a pitched battle, she could not be defeated in the war. All the same there was dissatisfaction, especially among the young men who found it hard to tolerate the thought of an invader being allowed to march where he liked.

Pericles himself was a friend of King Archidamus and he feared that either out of friendly feeling or in order to make him unpopular the King might leave untouched his own property in the country. So he informed the Athenians that if his estates and houses were not laid waste like those of other people, he proposed to give them up and make them public property.

Meanwhile the Peloponnesian army, after making some unsuccessful attacks on one of the frontier fortresses, moved into the plain near Eleusis and began to devastate the whole area. From there they went on to the rich farming district of Acharnae, only seven miles from Athens, and laid that waste. There was a large number of Acharnians in the Athenian army and they, as was natural, resented staying behind the walls and doing nothing while they could see the smoke rising from their own villages.

Pericles, however, was convinced of the rightness of his strategy and did not depart from it. While the Peloponnesians were still in Attica, he sent out a fleet of a hundred

Athenian triremes with a large body of troops to sail round
the Peloponnese. They were joined by fifty ships from
Corcyra and others from their allies in that area. They
captured or laid waste various places along the coast, won
over the large island of Cephallenia without striking a blow
and then sailed back to Athens. All this time other squadrons
were operating along the eastern trade routes and in Thrace
and there were still three thousand Athenian heavy infantry
besieging Potidaea.

When their supplies were exhausted the army of Sparta
and her allies marched home. They were needed both for
getting in the harvest (since they, unlike Athens, did not
depend on imports) and in order to defend their own country.
As soon as they had gone, in the autumn, Pericles led out
the whole Athenian army and invaded the territory of
Sparta's ally, Megara. The fleet was returning at the same
time and joined in the operation. This was the largest
Athenian army that had ever yet taken the field. There were
ten thousand citizen heavy infantry, three thousand from
the resident aliens and numbers of cavalry and light armed
troops. The people of Megara could only retire behind their
fortifications and watch the devastation of their country.
These invasions of the Megarid occurred for year after year,
and in general much the same pattern of warfare by land and
sea was repeated for some years to come. In this first year of
the war no decision had been reached, but the Athenians
could reasonably claim that they had done more harm to
their enemies than they had suffered themselves.

4. Pericles' Funeral Speech

IN the winter following the invasion the Athenians gave a public funeral for those who had been the first to die in the war. These funerals, which are held annually, are done as follows: two days before the ceremony the bones of the fallen are brought and put in a tent which has been erected and people make what offerings they wish to their own dead. Then there is a funeral procession in which coffins of cypress wood are carried on wagons. There is one empty bier in the procession: this is for the missing, whose bodies could not be recovered. Everyone who wishes, both citizens and foreigners, can join in the procession and the women who are related to the dead are there to make their lament at the tomb. The bones are laid in the public burial place, which is in the most beautiful quarter outside the city walls. The only exception is those who died at Marathon, who, because their achievement was considered absolutely outstanding, were buried on the battlefield itself.

After the bones have been laid in the earth, a man chosen by the city for his intelligence and his general reputation makes a speech in praise of the dead, and after the speech all depart. This is the traditional procedure at Athens and all through the war the Athenians followed this ancient custom. Now, at this first funeral of the war, the man chosen to make the speech was Pericles. When the moment arrived, he came forward from the tomb and spoke from a high platform, so that he might be heard by as many people as possible.

In praising the dead he spoke first of all of what they had died to defend—the greatness, the beauty and the originality of Athens. Among other things he said:

'Our system of government is our own. It would be truer to say that we are a model to others than that we imitate any-one else. We call our constitution a democracy, because with us power is in the hands, not of a minority, but of the whole people.

'In private matters everyone is equal before the law. In public affairs, when it is a question of putting power and responsibility into the hands of one man rather than another, what counts is not rank or money, but the ability to do the job well. No one is kept out of politics because he is poor. And just as our political life is free and open, so we are free and tolerant in our day-to-day lives. We do not get into a state with our next-door neighbour if he enjoys himself in his own way, nor do we give him the kind of black looks which, though they do no real harm, still do hurt people's feelings.

'We obey those whom we have appointed to positions of authority, and we obey the laws, especially those which are for the protection of the oppressed, and those unwritten laws which everyone knows it is shameful to break.

'We work hard, and when our work is over we have all kinds of means of recreating our spirits. Throughout the year there are festivals in which we all join, contests in poetry, drama, music and athletics; and the beauty of our public buildings is always in front of our eyes, while in our own homes we find a beauty and good taste which delight us every day and which drive away our cares.

'It is worth remembering some of the great differences between our way of life and that of our enemies. Take the question of military security. The Spartans have regular deportation of aliens and will go to any length to prevent people from finding out what are regarded as military secrets. But our city is open to all the world and everyone is free to look at what he likes in it. This is because we rely not on secret weapons, but on our own real courage and loyalty. There is a difference too in our educational systems. The Spartans, from their earliest boyhood, are made to go through the most strict and laborious training in courage. We pass our lives without all these restrictions, and yet we are just as ready to face danger as they are when the moment comes. And I think there are advantages in our way of meeting danger voluntarily, with an easy mind and with a courage that is natural rather than state-induced. We do not have to spend our time practising how to be brave; it comes to us naturally.

'Our love of what is beautiful does not lead to extravagance; our love of the things of the mind does not make us soft. We think of wealth as something to be properly used, not something to boast about. If any one of us is poor, he need not be ashamed to admit it; the real shame is in doing nothing practical about it. Here each one of us is interested not only in his own affairs, but in the affairs of the state as well. Everyone is well informed on general politics. And if we find a man who takes no interest in politics, we do not say that he is minding his own business; we say that he has no business here at all. Each one of us takes part in our decisions on policy and in discussion of them, since we consider that thought and action should go together. If we take risks, we have estimated them beforehand. Others are brave out of ignorance; and when they stop to think, they begin to fear. But the really brave man is the one who best knows what is sweet in life and what is terrible, and then goes out undeterred to meet what is to come.

'In making friends with other people we do not work out calculations of profit and loss; we act freely and liberally, without afterthought, preferring to do good than to receive it. Taking everything together, then, I declare that our city is an education to Greece, and I declare that in my opinion each single one of our citizens, in all the manifold aspects of life, is able to show himself the rightful lord and owner of his own person, and to do this, moreover, with exceptional grace and exceptional versatility. And here I am not boasting; I am simply stating facts. You need only think of what we have accomplished by these very qualities which I have mentioned. For our adventurous spirit has forced an entry into every sea and into every land; and everywhere we have left behind us everlasting memorials of good done to our friends or suffering inflicted on our enemies.

'This, then, is the kind of city for which these men, who could not bear the thought of losing her, nobly fought and nobly died. We who remain behind may hope to be spared their fate, but must resolve to keep the same daring spirit against the foe. It is not simply a question of estimating how much we stand to gain or lose by victory or defeat. You know all about this as well as I do. What I would prefer is that you should fix your eyes every day on the greatness of Athens as she really is, and should fall in love with her. When you realise her greatness, then reflect that what made her great was men with a spirit of adventure, men who knew their duty, men who were ashamed to fall below a certain standard. If ever they failed in an enterprise, they made up their minds that at any rate the city should not find their courage lacking to her, and they gave to her the best contribution that they could. They gave her their lives, to her and to all of us, and for their own selves they won praises that never grow old, the most splendid of sepulchres—not the sepulchres in which their bodies are laid, but where their glory remains eternal in men's minds, always there on the right occasion to stir others to speech or to action. For famous men have the whole earth as their memorial: it is not only the inscriptions on their graves in their own country that mark them out; no, in foreign lands also, not in any visible form but in people's hearts, their memory abides and grows. It is for you to try to be like them. Make up your minds that happiness depends on being free, and freedom depends on being courageous. Let there be no relaxation in face of the perils of the war.'

5. The Second Year of the War. The Plague and its Effects

AT the beginning of the following summer the Spartans and their allies again invaded Attica. They had not been there many days before the plague broke out, first in the harbour town of Piraeus and soon afterwards in the city of Athens.

This was a catastrophe which had entered into nobody's calculations. It was utterly unexpected and for that reason all the more damaging. At the beginning the doctors were quite incapable of treating the disease, because it was something altogether new to them. In fact mortality among the doctors was the highest of all, since they came in more frequent contact with the sick. Nor was any other human art or science of any help at all. Equally useless were prayers made in the temples, consultation of oracles and so forth;

indeed in the end people were so overcome by their sufferings that they ceased to pay any attention to such things.

It is said that the plague started in Ethiopia and then spread into North Africa and the Near East. But no one so far has been able to explain its origin or give the reasons for its powerful effects. I myself shall merely describe what it was like, and set down the symptoms, knowledge of which will enable it to be recognised if it should ever break out again. I had the disease myself and saw others suffering from it.

That year there happened to be much less of any other kind of sickness than usual, though all who did have any illness ended by catching the plague. But in other cases there seemed no reason for the attacks. People in perfect health suddenly began to have burning feelings in the head; their eyes became red and inflamed; inside their mouths there was bleeding from the throat and tongue, and the breath became unnatural and unpleasant. The next symptoms were sneezing and hoarseness of voice, pains in the chest and coughing. Next, the stomach was affected with stomach-aches and with painful vomitings of every kind of bile. Usually there were also attacks of ineffectual retching, producing violent spasms; these symptoms sometimes ended with this stage of the disease, but sometimes continued long after. Externally the body was not very hot to the touch, nor was there any pallor: the skin was rather reddish and livid, breaking out into small pustules and ulcers. But under the skin there was a constant burning sensation. People could not bear the touch of the lightest linen clothing; they wanted to be completely naked or to plunge into cold water.

Many of those who were uncared for actually did so, plunging into the water tanks in an attempt to relieve their thirst, though it made no difference whether they drank much or little. And then all the time they suffered from insomnia and the desperate feeling of not being able to keep still.

The body showed surprising powers of resistance to all the agony. Often there was still some strength left on the seventh or eighth day, which was the time when, in most cases, death came. But if people survived this critical period, then the disease descended to the bowels, producing violent ulceration and uncontrollable diarrhoea, so that most of them died later as the result of the weakness caused by this. For the disease, which had started in the head, went on to affect every part of the body in turn, ending up by fastening on the extremities of the body. It affected the genitals, the fingers and the toes, and many of those who recovered lost the use of these members. Others too, when they first began to get better, suffered from a total loss of memory, not knowing who they were themselves and being unable to recognise their friends. There were others also who went blind.

Words indeed fail me when I try to give a general picture of this disease and also when I try to describe the sufferings of individuals, which seemed almost beyond the capacity of human nature to endure.

The most terrible thing of all was the despair into which people fell when they realised that they had caught the plague. They would immediately adopt an attitude of utter hopelessness, and, by giving in in this way, would lose their powers of resistance. It was terrible too to see people dying like sheep through having caught the disease as a result of nursing others. There were many who were afraid to visit the sick, so that whole households died with no one to look after them. But those who felt ashamed to leave their friends unattended and made it a point of honour to act properly usually lost their own lives. Yet still the ones who felt most pity for the sick and dying were those who had had the plague themselves and had recovered from it. They knew what it was like and at the same time felt themselves to be safe, since no one caught the disease twice, or, if he did, the second attack was never fatal. Such people were congratulated on all sides, and they themselves were so elated at the time of their recovery that they foolishly imagined that they could never die of any other disease in the future.

What made things still worse than they would have been was the overcrowding as a result of the removal of people from the country into the city. There were no houses for the incomers; they lived in badly ventilated huts during the whole hot season and they died like flies. The bodies of the dying were heaped one on top of the other, and half-dead creatures could be seen staggering about in the streets or flocking around the fountains trying to quench their thirst. The temples, where many had taken up their quarters, were full of the dead bodies of people who had died inside them. The catastrophe was so overwhelming that no one knew what would happen next and people became indifferent to laws and to religion. Funeral ceremonies became disorganised and people buried their dead as best they could. Often there had been so many deaths already in a household that the survivors had no means for a proper burial and, out of indifference or shamelessness, they would either put the corpse they were carrying on a pyre prepared for someone else's funeral and set it alight, or just throw it on to another pyre that was already burning.

Because of the plague a quite new state of lawlessness and lack of restraint began to grow in Athens. Seeing how uncertain life was from one moment to another, people decided to spend their money quickly and spend it on pleasure, since it seemed that neither money or life would be theirs for long. As for what is called honour, no one paid any attention to it, so doubtful did it seem whether one would survive to enjoy the reputation for it. It was generally agreed that the only thing that mattered was the pleasure of the moment. No fear of god or law of man had a restraining influence. As for the gods, it seemed to be the same thing whether one worshipped them or not, when one saw the good and the bad dying indiscriminately. As for breaking the law, no one expected to live long enough to be punished for it.

Meanwhile, with men dying inside the city, the Spartan army continued to ravage the countryside. As before Pericles kept the Athenian army inside the walls, but took a force of a hundred ships with four thousand heavy infantry and three hundred cavalry to ravage the coasts of the Peloponnese. This force returned after the Spartans had retired and was then sent north under Hagnon, another general, to join in the operations still going on against Potidaea. But the plague broke out among Hagnon's men too, and they infected the army at Potidaea which up to then had been free from the disease. After forty days Hagnon returned to Athens, having lost one-quarter of his army. And throughout the summer men continued to die in the city and in Piraeus.

6. Pericles Justifies his Policy

THE Athenians had now had their land twice devastated and had to contend with the plague at the same time. A change came over their spirit and they began to blame Pericles for having persuaded them to go to war and hold him responsible for all their misfortunes. They became eager to make peace and actually sent ambassadors to Sparta who did not succeed in achieving anything. So now all their angry feelings turned against Pericles.

Pericles saw how they felt: he saw, in fact, that they were behaving exactly as he had expected that they would. So he called an assembly and spoke to his fellow-citizens with the aim of putting fresh courage into them and leaving them in a calmer and more confident frame of mind. He told them that he had expected this outbreak of anger against him, since he understood the reasons for it and he went on to point out that what he had always said was still true—that the safety and happiness of each individual depended on the safety and happiness of the state as a whole. He then discussed the particular situation in which they were and their irresolution in giving in both to their sufferings and to the enemy. He said:

'If one has a free choice and can live undisturbed, of course it is sheer folly to go to war. But if the choice is forced upon one—submission and immediate slavery or else danger with the hope of survival—then I prefer the man who stands up to danger rather than the one who runs away from it. As for me, I am the same as I was and do not alter; it is you who have changed. Now that a great and sudden disaster has fallen on you, you have weakened in carrying out to the end the resolutions which you made. When things happen suddenly, unexpectedly and against all calculation, it takes the heart out of a man; and this certainly has happened to you, with the plague coming on top of everything else. Yet still you must remember that you are citizens of a great city and that you were brought up in a way of life suited to her greatness; you must therefore be willing to face any disaster which may come and be determined never to sacrifice the glory that is yours. Each of you must try to stifle his own particular sorrow as he joins with the rest in working for the safety of us all.

'And if you think that our war-time sufferings may grow greater and greater and still not bring us any nearer to victory, you ought to be satisfied with the arguments I have used before. Here is another argument which is a valid one, but which I have not mentioned before. In fact, since it looks rather like boasting, I should not mention it now if it were not that I see that your feelings of discouragement are quite unreasonable. Now, when you think of your empire, you think it consists simply of your allies; but I have something else to tell you. The whole world before our eyes can be divided into two parts, the land and the sea, each of which is valuable and useful to man. Of the whole of one of these parts you are in control—not only of the seas your ships sail now, but elsewhere too, if you want to go further. With your navy as it is today there is no power on earth—not the King of Persia nor any people under the sun—which can stop you from sailing where you wish. Mastery of the seas is the source and basis of your power and compared with this houses and cultivated land are of very minor importance, no more to be valued than gardens and other luxuries that go with wealth. So long as we preserve our freedom by being willing to fight for it, we shall soon regain these other things. But if we lose our freedom, we shall lose everything.

'When you go forward against the enemy, you should be animated not only by courage but by a real sense of your superiority. There is a kind of confidence which springs from a mixture of ignorance and good luck and can be felt even by cowards; but this sense of superiority comes only to those who, like us, have real and solid reasons for knowing that they are better placed than their enemies.

'You are wrong to be angry with me, you who came to the same conclusions as I did about the necessity for making war. Certainly the enemy have invaded our country and done as one might have expected they would do, once you refused to give in to them; and then the plague, something we did not expect, fell upon us. In fact out of everything else this has been the only case of something happening which we did not anticipate. And it is largely because of this that I have become unpopular, quite unfairly, unless you are also going to give me the credit for every piece of good luck that may come our way. But the right thing to do is always this: to endure what the gods send and to face one's enemies with courage. This was the old Athenian way: do not let any action of yours prevent it from still being so.

'Remember that the reason why Athens has the greatest name in all the world is because she has never given in to adversity, but has spent more life and labour in warfare than any other state, thus winning the greatest power that has ever existed in history, a power that will be remembered for ever. And even if (since all things are born to decay) there should come a time when we are forced to yield, yet still it will be remembered that of all Hellenic powers we held the widest sway over the Hellenes, that we stood firm in the greatest wars against their combined forces and against individual states, that we lived in a city which had been perfectly equipped in every direction and was the greatest in Hellas.

'All who have taken it upon themselves to rule over others have incurred hatred and unpopularity for a time: but if one has a great aim to pursue, this burden of envy must be accepted, and it is wise to accept it. Hatred does not last for long; but the brilliance of the present is the glory of the future stored up for ever in the memory of man. It is for you to safeguard that future glory and to do nothing now that is dishonourable. Now, then, is the time to show your energy. Do not send embassies to Sparta: do not give the impression that you are weakening under your present sufferings! To face calamity with a mind as unclouded as may be, and quickly to react against it—that, in a city and in an individual, is real strength.'

In this way Pericles tried to stop the Athenians from being angry with him and to raise their spirits above their sufferings. So far as public policy went he was successful. They sent no more embassies to Sparta and carried on the war with vigour. But they still felt their sufferings. The rich had lost their fine estates in the country; the poor, who had little enough to start with, had lost even that. And on top of all this there was the plague. They were not satisfied until they had found someone, not themselves, to blame, and so they condemned Pericles to pay a fine. Not long afterwards, as is the way with crowds, they changed their minds. They re-elected Pericles to the generalship and put all their affairs into his hands, knowing that he was the best man they had. This was perfectly true. During the whole period of peacetime when Pericles was the leading statesman the city had been wisely led and it was under him that Athens was at her greatest. He too was a victim of the plague and only survived the outbreak of the war for two years and six months, and after his death it became clear how accurate had been his estimate of Athens' strength and how correct had been his policy.

He had said that Athens would be victorious if she bided her time and took care of her navy, if she avoided trying to add to her empire until the war was over and if she did nothing to risk the safety of the city herself. But his successors did the exact opposite.

Pericles, because of his position, his intelligence and his known integrity, could respect the liberty of the people and at the same time hold them in check. It was he who led them rather than they who led him, and, since he never sought power from any wrong motive, he was under no necessity of flattering them. He was so highly respected that he was able to speak angrily to them and contradict them. So, in what was nominally a democracy, power was really in the hands of the first citizen. But his successors, who were more on a level with each other, each aimed at being in the first place. They both feared the people and flattered them, and their personal ambitions led to a number of mistakes in general policy. Among these mistakes was the expedition against Sicily, though here the mistake was not so much an error in judgement about the opposition to be expected as a failure of the home government to give proper support to their forces overseas. Because they were so busy in their personal struggles for leadership they allowed this expedition to lose its impetus. The result was a disaster in which Athens lost most of her fleet and all her forces in Sicily. This led to a revolt of nearly all her allies and a revolution in Athens herself.

Yet even so Athens still held out for eight more years against her original enemies, who were now reinforced by the Sicilians, against most of her own allies and against the Persians who by this time had joined the other side and were helping Sparta with subsidies for her fleet. And in the end it was only because the Athenians had ruined themselves by quarrels among themselves that they were forced to surrender. So overwhelmingly great were the resources that Pericles had in mind at the time when he prophesied an easy victory for Athens over Sparta and her allies alone.

7. Siege of Plataea. Victories of Phormio. Revolt of Mytilene

IN the winter of this second year of the war the Athenians finally overcame the resistance of Potidaea. The people there were starving, and among the horrors which starvation brings there were actually cases of cannibalism. So they entered into negotiations for the surrender of their city and the Athenian generals, who were themselves in an exposed position and who knew that Athens had already spent great sums of money on the campaign, granted generous terms. The people of Potidaea with their wives and children were allowed to go free, the men taking one garment and the women two, and also a fixed sum of money for their journey. Later the Athenians sent out colonists of their own and resettled the place. At Athens the generals were blamed for not having enforced stricter terms.

Early in the next year, the third of the war, King Archidamus and the army of Sparta and her allies, instead of invading Attica, marched against the city of Plataea. Before they had begun to lay waste the land, the Plataeans sent representatives to him and reminded him of how Pausanias, the Spartan commander, and all the other Greeks who had won the victory against the Persians at Plataea had bound themselves by oaths that Plataea should be free and independent for ever and that if she were at any time the victim of aggression they had promised to come to her aid. 'And now,' the Plataeans said, 'you are acting clean contrary to your oaths. You have allied yourselves with the Thebans, who have always been our bitterest enemies, and you are making an unprovoked attack on our land.'

At this point Archidamus interrupted them. According to his argument it was not the Spartans, but the Plataeans, who were being false to their oaths. Sparta and her allies were fighting to liberate Greece from the tyranny of Athens. If Plataea were to join in this good work, or even remain neutral, she would have nothing to fear.

The Plataeans of course realised that, in any event, they had a great deal to fear, if not from Sparta, then certainly from their hereditary enemies, the Thebans, who had already once tried to occupy their city in peacetime. Up to now their only effective guarantee of independence had been their alliance with Athens. Moreover, their wives and children were already in Athens for safety and in order to leave only fighting men in a city that might at any time be besieged. So, after discussing the Spartan offer and sending a deputation to Athens, they informed King Archidamus that it was impossible for them to do as he had suggested.

Archidamus made a solemn appeal to the gods and heroes of the land of Plataea to bear witness that he was acting in no spirit of aggression. He then brought his army into action. Every attempt was made that year to break down the resistance of the Plataeans and every attempt failed. The defenders were very few. Inside the city there were only four hundred Plataeans with eighty Athenians and one hundred and ten women to do the cooking for the garrison. This small force held out against all assaults, rebuilding the walls wherever they were in danger of being breached. The most serious attack came from an attempt to set the whole city on fire. Vast quantities of faggots were brought up to the walls, covered with sulphur and pitch and set alight. There was an enormous blaze and, if the wind had risen, as the attackers had hoped, the Plataeans could not possibly have survived. However there was a sudden thunderstorm and a heavy fall of rain and this saved the city.

After this last failure the Spartans dismissed most of their army and kept just enough troops to build a wall all round the city so as to block it off from all supplies. They now aimed at starving the garrison into surrender. And so the siege began.

During the same summer the Athenian admiral Phormio was in the Gulf of Corinth with a squadron of twenty ships. His duty was to guard the port of Naupactus, on the northern shore of the Gulf. Naupactus was invaluable to the

Athenians, since it gave them control of the Gulf. This control was now threatened by an attempt by Sparta and her allies to achieve something by sea. They fought two engagements with Phormio and each time had the advantage of greatly superior numbers, since the reinforcements which should have reached Phormio before the battle were delayed in Crete. In the first battle his twenty ships utterly routed a Peloponnesian force of forty-seven ships. In the second battle the odds were even greater—seventy-seven against the same Athenian twenty. Here too, though the enemy ships did well at the beginning of the battle, they were finally routed. The Spartans found these Athenian victories difficult to explain. They thought that victories on the sea were won in the same way as victories on land and that if a large naval force were defeated by a much smaller one, it must be because of cowardice. They had not yet learnt how important training and experience are in naval matters and both the tactics and the seamanship of the Athenians were still mysteries to them.

In the second of the two engagements against Phormio the fleet of Sparta and her allies had had the advantage of the resolute and intelligent leadership of a young Spartan, Brasidas, a man of great energy and an ability to act quickly which is rare among Spartans. The men under his command had fought well and had only lost the battle because in the moment of victory they had become over-excited and careless, thus giving the Athenians, with their long experience, an opportunity to turn the tables. But in the next two years the Spartan naval commanders by their hesitation and over-caution lost the first real chances they had had of inflicting a serious blow on Athenian sea power.

This chance came in the fourth year of the war when the large island of Lesbos, which still provided a fleet of her own, revolted from the Athenian alliance. The revolt was led by Mytilene, the largest city on the island, and was organised by the party of the oligarchs, who here as elsewhere were pro-Spartan, while the democrats were pro-Athenian. News of the plot soon reached Athens and so the revolt broke out earlier than had been intended. The Athenians immediately sent out forty ships and proceeded to blockade the two harbours of Mytilene. The rebels naturally appealed to Sparta for help.

They made their appeal in August, after the Spartans and their allies had already made their yearly invasion of Attica, and they pointed out that here was a magnificent opportunity for the Spartan alliance. If a part, and a very important part, of the Athenian empire were able to revolt successfully, other states would soon follow the example. Moreover, Athens had been seriously weakened by the plague and her resources were fully stretched. She already had seventy ships at sea—thirty operating against the Peloponnese and forty at Mytilene—and if a combined sea and land operation were launched against her, she would be very seriously threatened and, at the very least, would have to withdraw from Lesbos.

It was a good argument and the Spartans decided to act on it. They called on their allies for troops for another invasion of Attica, promised naval help to Mytilene and planned to transport ships across the isthmus of Corinth into Athenian waters.

However the allied troops came in slowly and reluctantly, not liking to be interrupted in the work of getting in the harvest. And the Athenians, so far from withdrawing any of their naval forces, manned another hundred ships with their own citizens and used this fleet to ravage the eastern coasts of the Peloponnese. This vigorous action alarmed the Spartans, who called off the invasion and postponed any serious naval action until the next year. All they did to help Mytilene was to send an officer of their own, Salaethus, into the place as an adviser.

Salaethus arrived during the winter. He found that the Athenians, under their commander, Paches, had immensely improved their position. In Mytilene itself food was running short and there was considerable discontent among the people. It appeared that the only hope was in breaking out through the Athenian lines and, on the advice of Salaethus, arms were issued to the citizens for this purpose. Obviously he misjudged the situation. As soon as the people were armed, they turned against the party of the oligarchs, and threatened to surrender the city to the Athenians. The oligarchs, finding themselves in a hopeless position, then made their own terms with Paches. The best they could get was that they should send envoys to Athens and leave the decision to the Athenians themselves.

A week after the surrender the Spartan admiral, Alcidas, with forty-two ships, who had made a slow and timorous voyage across the Aegean, arrived without having been observed by Paches' fleet. Instead of taking action either in Lesbos or elsewhere, he immediately fled back to the Peloponnese, pursued by Paches' ships, who had been informed first that he had arrived and then that he had run away. Indeed the only action that Alcidas took was to massacre most of the prisoners whom he had taken on his voyage. He was only prevented from killing all of them by some exiles from Samos, who pointed out that to massacre all Greeks who fell into his hands was not the best way of convincing the others of the sincerity of Sparta's claim that the war was fought for the liberation of Hellas.

After he had gone Paches arrested those members of the oligarchical party who seemed to have been most active in the revolt and sent them with Salaethus to Athens. The Mytilenian envoys were already there and were waiting to be heard.

8. The Debate on Mytilene

THROUGH their own slowness and through the cowardice or incompetence of Alcidas, Sparta had missed a great opportunity. But the Athenians, though they had reacted vigorously and escaped from what might have been a very difficult position, realised how great the danger had been and were now in a mood of extreme and bitter anger.

Salaethus had been put to death, even though he had promised to arrange to have the Peloponnesian army withdrawn from Plataea. Now the Athenians decided to put to death the entire adult male population of Mytilene and to make slaves of the women and children. That Mytilene, which was an allied and not a subject state, like the others, should have revolted seemed to them unendurable. So they sent out a trireme to Paches with orders to put to death the Mytileneans immediately.

But next day there was a change of feeling. People began to think how cruel a decision this was—to destroy not only the guilty, but the whole population of a state. Another assembly was called and the question was debated for the second time.

Various opinions were expressed on both sides. In favour of the original decision the chief speaker was Cleon, a man remarkable for the violence and self-assurance of his character. At this time, after the death of Pericles, he had far the greatest influence over the mass of the people and it was he who had been chiefly responsible for persuading them to vote as they had done at the last assembly. The speech he made now was characteristic of him.

'I have noticed,' he said, 'often enough already that a democracy is incapable of governing others, and I am all the more convinced of this when I see how you are changing your minds about the people of Mytilene. What you fail to see is that when you give way to your feelings of compassion, you are guilty of a kind of weakness which is dangerous to you and which will not make other people any more fond of you than they are already. The fact is that your empire is a dictatorship exercised over subjects who do not like it and who would always revolt if they thought they could do so with any chance of success. Your authority does not depend on any good will of theirs, but simply and solely on your superior strength.

'And this is the worst thing of all—to pass measures and then not abide by them. We should realise that a city is better off with bad laws, so long as they remain fixed, than with good laws that are constantly being altered, that ordinary common sense is a good deal more helpful than abstract theories, and that as a rule states are better governed by the man in the street than by intellectuals.

'Personally I am amazed that anyone should want to re-open this question of Mytilene. Is someone going to contradict me and say that the harm done to us by the Mytileneans was really a good thing for us? And are you going to listen to that sort of argument? The trouble with you is that you enjoy listening to these so-called clever speakers. You have become regular speech-goers and it never occurs to you that these intellectuals whom you enjoy listening to have either been bribed to say what they are saying or are simply showing off among themselves.

'Now look at the facts. I say that Mytilene has treated you worse than any state has ever done. I could make allowances for people who revolt against an intolerable government, but we have treated Mytilene exceptionally well. They had their own fleet, their own fortifications, their own government. To act as they acted is not what I should call a revolt; it is a case of calculated aggression. The fact is that we treated them much too well. What we should have done long ago was to treat them in exactly the same way as all the rest; then they would never have grown so arrogant; for it is a general rule of human nature that people despise those who treat them well and look up to those who make no concessions. Let them now therefore have the punishment which their crime deserves. Do not put the blame on the aristocracy and say that the people were innocent. The fact is that they were all in the revolt together at the beginning.

'Let there be no hope held out to them that we, either as a result of a good speech or a large bribe, are likely to forgive them on the grounds that it is only human to make mistakes. Do not alter the decision you have already made. To feel pity, to be carried away by the pleasure of hearing a clever argument, to listen to the claims of decency are three things that are entirely against the interests of an imperial power. Do not be guilty of them.

'To sum the whole thing up, I say that, if you follow my advice, you will be doing the right thing as far as Mytilene is concerned and at the same time will be acting in your own interests; if you act differently, you will not win them over, but will be passing judgement on yourselves. For if they were justified in revolting, you must be wrong in holding power. If, however, whatever the rights and wrongs may be, you propose to hold power all the same, then your interest demands that these too, rightly or wrongly, must be punished. The only alternative is to surrender your empire, so that you can afford to go in for philanthropy.

'Punish these people as they deserve and make an example of them to your other allies, plainly showing that revolt will be punished by death.'

After Cleon's speech another statesman, Diodotus, who had opposed the decision of the previous assembly, rose to answer him.

'I do not agree with Cleon,' he said, 'when he suggests that it is a bad thing to have frequent discussions on things that are important. Bad decisions can be reached under the influence of hate and anger, and a bad decision should not be irrevocable. And anyone who maintains that words cannot be a guide to action must be either a fool or a knave; he is a fool if he imagines that one can estimate the uncertainties of the future by any other medium; and he is a knave if, knowing that he cannot put up a good argument for what he wants, he stifles argument altogether.

'Now let us look at the question of Mytilene dispassionately and with a view to deciding what is best for ourselves; for the important thing is our own future, not whether other people happen to be guilty or happen to be innocent. Suppose that they are the most guilty people in the world; it does not follow that I should propose the death penalty, unless that were in your interest. Suppose that they deserve to be forgiven; I should still not recommend forgiveness unless that were the best thing for the state. What we should consider is the future, not the past or the present.

'Cleon's chief point is that to inflict the death penalty will be useful to us since it will act as a deterrent to other cities who may be thinking of revolt. I disagree with him entirely.

'If you think of the history of punishment in human societies, you will find that the death penalty has been laid down for many offences less serious than this one. Yet people still take risks, when they think they can get away with it. No one commits a crime which he does not think he can carry out successfully. The same is true of states. Cities and individuals alike, all are by nature disposed to do wrong, and there is no law that will prevent it. Even when everyone knows that the penalty for certain crimes is death, these crimes are still committed. Either, therefore, we must discover some fear more potent than the fear of death, or we must admit that here certainly we have not got an adequate deterrent. Under the stress of poverty, or moved by insolence and pride or some other master passion, men will always be impelled into unlawful acts. Hope will conceive the project; desire will persuade them that it will be successful—invisible factors, but more powerful than the terrors that are obvious to our eyes.

'So do not allow yourselves to make the wrong decision because of a mistaken belief in the effectiveness of capital punishment. If you deprive rebels of all possibility of repenting and atoning for what they have done, you will be merely heaping up more trouble for yourselves. At the moment, if a city has revolted and sees that the revolt cannot succeed, it will pay an indemnity and will continue to be useful to you. But if Cleon's method is adopted, there will be no point in ever coming to terms. Since there will be no hope anyway of forgiveness, the rebels will fight to the last and when you recover the city, it will be in ruins and useless to you.

'And yet the whole strength of our empire depends on the resources of our subjects. What we should realise is that the proper basis of our security is good administration rather than the fear of legal penalties. The right way to deal with free people is this—not to inflict enormous punishments on them after they have revolted, but to take enormous care to see that this point is never reached, to give them no reason to contemplate the idea of revolt.

'And there is another point where Cleon is entirely mistaken. As things are now, in all the cities the democracy is friendly to you. Either it is in control, in which case there is no revolt; or, if it is forced to join the oligarchies in revolting, it remains secretly hostile to them, so that you always have the people on your side. So it was in Mytilene. The democratic party had nothing to do with the revolt and when they got arms into their hands, they voluntarily gave the city up to you. But if you do what Cleon wants and put the whole population to death, you will first of all be punishing your friends, and secondly you will be doing just what the reactionary classes want most, since in future revolts the people will have nothing to gain from opposing them.

'In asking you to approve my proposal, I am not asking you to be swayed too much by pity or by ordinary decent feelings. I, no more than Cleon, wish you to be influenced by such emotions. I propose that you try at your leisure the people whom Paches has considered guilty and has sent to Athens and that you allow the rest to live in their own city. In following this course you will be acting wisely for the future and will be doing something which will make your enemies fear you now. For those who make wise decisions are more formidable than those who rush madly into strong action.'

After this speech there was still much conflict of opinion, and when there was a show of hands the votes on each side were nearly equal. In the end, however, the motion of Diodotus was passed.

Another trireme was sent out immediately to Mytilene and the crew made all the haste they could. They feared that unless they caught up with the first trireme, which had a start of about twenty-four hours, they would arrive only to find that the whole population had been put to death. The ambassadors from Mytilene provided wine and barley for the crew and promised great rewards if they arrived in time, and the men made all the speed they could; they kept on rowing continually, taking it in turn to sleep. Luckily they had no wind against them and, as the first ship was not hurrying on its distasteful mission, it only arrived just in front of the second ship. Paches had just time to read the orders and prepare to carry them out when the second ship put into harbour and prevented the massacre. So narrow had been the escape of Mytilene.

Afterwards the other Mytileneans, who had been sent to Athens by Paches as those chiefly responsible for the revolt, were put to death on the motion of Cleon. There were about a thousand of them. The fortifications of Mytilene were destroyed and the Athenians took over their navy and all the towns on the mainland which had been under their control. So for the future the Mytileneans became subjects of Athens.

9. End of Plataea.
Revolution in Corcyra

IN the same summer, and after the conquest of Mytilene, the defenders of Plataea were forced by hunger to surrender to the Spartans. By this time the garrison numbered only about two hundred Plataeans and twenty-five Athenians. The rest had managed to escape through the Spartan lines during a stormy rainy night in the middle of the winter. The escape had been brilliantly organised and nearly all who took part in it got away safely to Athens. There were one hundred and twelve of them all told. They had crossed two circles of walls and then eluded a large pursuing force, not only saving their own lives but enabling the rest of the garrison to hold out longer on the small supplies of food that were left.

Now, however, they had been too much weakened by hunger to resist longer. They accepted the Spartan offer that they should surrender and abide by the judgement of Spartan judges on the understanding that the guilty should be punished, but all should have a fair trial.

They were then given food by the Spartans for a few days until the judges from Sparta arrived. When the judges came, the Plataeans were called forward and asked simply this one question: 'Have you done anything to help the Spartans and their allies in this present war?'

The Plataeans had expected something very different from this and asked permission to state their case more fully. This was granted and their spokesman pointed out that they had been attacked first by their old enemies, the Thebans, and then by the Spartans. They had then defended themselves. Obviously they could not say that in doing so they had been helping the Spartans and their allies, and if their fate was to depend on their answer to the Spartan question, it seemed that they had been already condemned in advance and that this was by no means the fair trial which they had been promised. They claimed that they had deserved better treatment than this. At the time of the Persian wars they had been the only state north of Attica which had not gone over to the Persians. At the final battle of Plataea they had fought side by side with the Spartans, whereas the Thebans had fought against them. After the war they, like Athens, had sent troops to help Sparta when she was in the greatest danger as a result of the earthquake and the revolt of the helots. Later still, when they were being attacked by Thebes, they had applied to Sparta for help and Sparta had told them to ask help from the Athenians because they were nearer. In short their record had been honourable from first to last. And now, they said, Sparta enjoyed among the Greeks the reputation for faith and honour and she claimed to be fighting this war for the liberation of Hellas. How could she enjoy this reputation or make this claim if she were now going to abandon those who had trusted her and who had always fought for Hellas as a whole to their bitterest enemies, the Thebans?

If the Spartan judges were moved at all by this appeal, they were more moved by the reflection that the Thebans had a large army and were among the most useful of their allies in the war against Athens. They replied that all the oaths they had sworn and all the pledges they had given to Plataea in the past had been on the assumption that Plataea would remain neutral. But she had sided with the enemies of Sparta and therefore Sparta felt herself no longer bound by the promises she had made.

So the Plataeans were again brought forward one by one and each was asked: 'Have you done anything to help the Spartans and their allies in the war?' As each man replied 'No,' he was taken away and put to death. All the two hundred Plataeans and the twenty-five Athenians were killed in this way. The women were made slaves, and the city was razed to the ground. On its site a large hotel was built. For the building operations the roofs and doors of the Plataeans were used. The land was made over to the Thebans. This was the end of Plataea.

Already this war had been marked by many acts of savagery, often performed, as in the case of the Plataeans, under a cover of justice and fair play. And now still more savage massacres and acts of reprisal began to take place in city after city as the result of civil war between parties of democrats, who would call in the support of Athens, and oligarchs, who would rely on Spartan help. One of the first and bitterest of these struggles took place in Corcyra at about this time.

Both Corinth and Sparta naturally wanted to detach Corcyra from her alliance with Athens and they did all they could to support the party of oligarchs inside the island. The leaders of this party, who had been heavily fined by the democrats, attempted to seize power by breaking into the Council chamber armed with daggers and murdering some sixty of their leading opponents. It was in order to support this party of the oligarchs that Sparta sent out Alcidas with fifty-three ships to Corcyra, soon after his flight across the Aegean from Lesbos. This time Alcidas had sailing with him as adviser the extremely competent Spartan Brasidas, but it seems that even Brasidas was unable to produce confidence or discipline in the fleet or courage in its admiral.

Before this fleet arrived, fighting had broken out in Corcyra and a small Athenian squadron of twelve ships had reached the island under the command of Nicostratus. In the fighting the democrats had had the advantage, but Nicostratus attempted to bring the two parties together and arrange a settlement under which there would be no reprisals. His aim was to encourage a government which would remain loyal to Athens and would not weaken itself by splitting into factions, and under his influence some sort of an agreement was reached, though in fact both parties were still looking for an opportunity to come out on top. While Nicostratus was there the democrats felt safe and, in spite of his efforts to restrain them, they arrested and interned some four hundred of the leading oligarchs.

It was at this point that Alcidas with his fifty-three ships arrived. His arrival caused panic and confusion among the Corcyraeans, who were faced with a large enemy fleet and were at the same time bitterly divided among themselves. However, they managed to man sixty ships and sent them out in a hurried and disorderly way, paying no attention to the advice of the Athenians, which was to let them sail out first and then to come up in support with all their ships together. As it was, the Corcyraean ships were soon in difficulty. Two of them immediately deserted and in some of the others fighting broke out among the crews. Nothing was done in order. The Spartans, when they saw what was happening, detached twenty of their ships to deal with the Corcyraeans and with the rest of their fleet bore down on the twelve Athenian ships. Considering the number of the enemy and the risk of encirclement, the Athenians did not attack the enemy in the centre. They attacked one wing of his line and sank one ship before turning back to renew the attack. After this the Spartans formed their ships into a circle and the Athenians rowed round them, trying to compress the circle so that the ships would fall foul of each other. This was what Phormio had done in the first battle at Naupactus and the result had been disastrous to the Spartans. So now they withdrew the twenty ships that had been dealing with the Corcyraeans and sailed against the twelve

Athenian ships with their entire fleet. The Athenians, taking their time, began to back water and withdraw. They carried out the manoeuvre slowly and in good order, wishing to give what was left of the Corcyraean fleet the chance to get back safely to harbour. In this way the fighting went on till sunset, with the Athenians covering the retreat of their allies and the Spartans showing no great eagerness to engage them. At sunset the Spartans withdrew, taking with them the thirteen Corcyraean ships which they had captured.

Next day Brasidas urged Alcidas to follow up his victory and sail again against the city, where by this time the democratic party were in a state bordering on panic. But Alcidas was not to be persuaded into taking any resolute action, even when the prospects before him were so good. He spent the day in laying waste some of the undefended parts of the island. At nightfall he was informed by fire signals that a fleet of sixty Athenian ships was approaching. He fled back to the Peloponnese immediately, thus sealing the fate of the oligarchs in Corcyra.

This Athenian fleet was under the command of Eurymedon and had been sent out from Athens as soon as the news had arrived of the revolution in Corcyra and of the expedition of Alcidas. Now the democrats in Corcyra realised that they were safe and they immediately began to round up their enemies and kill them. Those who had been interned had taken refuge in the temple of Hera, but the democrats persuaded fifty of them to come out and be given a trial. They then condemned every one of them to death. Most of the others, who had refused to be tried, thereupon killed themselves there in the temple; some hanged themselves on the trees and others committed suicide in various other ways. During the seven days that Eurymedon stayed there with his sixty ships, the Corcyraeans continued to massacre those of their own citizens whom they considered to be their enemies. These were always accused of plotting against the democracy, but in fact many people were killed because of personal hatreds or by people who owed them money and did not want to pay it back. Before long men stopped at nothing. There were cases of fathers killing their sons and brothers killing brothers.

So savage was this revolution, and it seemed all the worse because it was one of the first that had broken out. Later, of course, the same things happened in city after city, with one side calling in the Athenians and the other the Spartans to help them. This sort of thing would have been impossible in peacetime, but in time of war each party could always depend on outside help to strengthen its own position and to do harm to its opponents.

These revolutions led to a general lowering of standards all over the Greek world. And to fit in with the change of events, words, too, had to change their usual meanings. What used to be called brutal aggression was now regarded as the courage one would expect to find in a party member; to favour moderation was another way of saying one was a coward; the ability to see both sides of a question meant that one was totally unfit for action. Fanatical enthusiasm was the mark of a real man and the ties of friendship or of family were weaker than the ties of party membership, since party members were ready to go to any extreme for any reason whatever.

Leaders of the parties both had programmes which looked admirable—on one side political equality for all citizens, on the other sound and honest administration—but in fact what each party was interested in was not the public good, but power for themselves.

The simple way of looking at things, which is so much a mark of a noble nature, was regarded as a ridiculous quality and soon ceased to exist. Society had become divided into two ideologically hostile camps and neither side trusted the other. In this state of mutual suspicion, no settlement seemed possible, since neither side could make any offer which the other side would believe to be sincere. So each side, thinking only of its own security, increased the insecurity of the other, and in the name of security the most monstrous acts of revenge and of oppression were carried out, as people were swept away by their ungovernable passions. The ordinary conventions of civilised life had broken down and human nature, which is always ready to do wrong even when laws exist, now showed itself in its true colours, as something incapable of controlling passion, insubordinate to the idea of justice, the enemy to anything superior to itself; for if it had not been for the pernicious power of envy, men would not so have exalted vengeance above innocence and profit above justice. Indeed it is true that in these displays of wanton revenge people begin to repeal those general laws of humanity which are there to give hope to all who are in distress. They do not reflect that a time may come when they too will be in danger and will need the protection of these laws.

After Eurymedon and his fleet had sailed away, the

democratic party remained in control in Corcyra. But some five hundred of their enemies had managed to escape and to occupy fortified posts in the interior of the island. Later they brought in mercenaries and took up a strong position on Mount Istome. Setting out from here, they overran much of the country districts and did all the damage they could to the people in the city. After two years an Athenian fleet again intervened and forced the party on the mountain to come to terms. The terms were that they should surrender to the judgement of the people of Athens, but that this agreement should be null and void if they made any attempt to escape before being taken to Athens. The democratic party in Corcyra feared that the Athenians might not put their enemies to death, and so they sent agents of their own to the prisoners who pretended to be their friends and told them that their only hope was in trying to escape, since the Athenian generals were going to hand them over to the people of Corcyra. The agents promised to provide them with boats and to help them. This story was believed by the prisoners, who did as they were told and attempted to escape; thus breaking their agreement. They were, of course, intercepted and now were in fact handed over to their enemies. About sixty of them, with their hands bound, were beaten and stabbed to death as they were forced to go between two lines of troops. The rest either killed themselves or were shot down with arrows or stoned to death.

It had been a great revolutionary struggle, but, so far as the period of the war is concerned, it was now over, since of the two parties, that of the oligarchs had practically ceased to exist.

10. Campaigns of Demosthenes. Pylos

AT the end of this same summer of the fifth year of the war the Athenians sent out a fleet of twenty ships to Sicily. In this island some of the great cities had been colonised by Ionians and some by Dorians. As was usual, the Ionians looked to Athens for help and support and the Dorians looked to Sparta. Up to this time none of the cities had given any practical help to either Athens or Sparta in the war, but the powerful city of Syracuse had been busy in adding to her own power by trying to subdue the Ionian cities in Sicily. The reason for the Athenian expedition was to give aid to their ally, Leontini, which was being attacked by Syracuse, to make sure that no supplies or reinforcements should reach Sparta from Sicily and at the same time to look into the general situation there and see whether it would be possible for them to gain control of the whole island. So this summer they fought with the people of Leontini against the Syracusans in various operations.

In the following winter there was another outbreak of the plague in Athens. In fact it had never entirely stopped, though after the first outbreak many fewer people had been affected by it. This second outbreak lasted for a whole year and the first outbreak had lasted for two years. Nothing did so much harm to Athens as the plague. In the regular army nearly five thousand heavy infantry and three hundred of the cavalry died of it, and in the general mass of the people no one ever discovered how many the deaths were.

Next summer, the sixth summer of the war, there was no Spartan invasion of Attica. The Spartan army had advanced to the Isthmus, but had then turned back because of the number of earthquakes which were taking place all over Greece. Meanwhile Athenian fleets were still operating in Sicily, in the Aegean and round the Peloponnese. Sixty ships, under the command of the experienced general, Nicias, had sailed against the island of Melos which, in spite of being an island, had refused to join the Athenian alliance. Nicias laid waste much of the island, but failed to win the place over.

In the same year two campaigns were fought in north-western Greece. In the first of these a force of Athenians and allies under Demosthenes suffered a severe defeat in rough country inland from Naupactus. After this a large force of Spartan allies under Spartan commanders made an attempt on Naupactus itself, hoping to find it undefended. However,

Demosthenes was still in the area. He had been afraid after his defeat to show himself in Athens and now he succeeded in putting enough men into Naupactus to make it safe. The Spartan army then turned northward and later in the year was ambushed and crushingly defeated by Demosthenes in spite of his being outnumbered and supported mostly by light-armed troops. This was the first defeat on land that the Spartans had suffered in the war. The Spartan commander and many of his officers were killed. Their successors, in order to save themselves, deserted their allies, whose supporting army was almost annihilated later. It was a great victory for Demosthenes and one which was extremely damaging to Spartan prestige. So ended the sixth year of the war.

In the next year Demosthenes was responsible for an even more spectacular success. In the early spring the Spartans and their allies had, as usual, invaded Attica and at about the same time the Athenians sent out forty ships to sail round the Peloponnese. This fleet was to call at Corcyra in order to help the democratic party in the city and then to go on to Sicily. Demosthenes, since his return, had no official position, but he received permission from the Athenians, at his own request, to make use of this fleet while it was off the Peloponnesian coast. His plan was to fortify a strong point on the coast and use this as a permanent base against Sparta. The place he selected was Pylos, which has a good harbour, is in a naturally strong position and is about forty-five miles from Sparta herself. It was, as events were to show, an excellent plan, but Demosthenes tried in vain to get the naval commanders, Eurymedon and

Sophocles, interested in it. They opposed the whole idea and told him that, if he wanted to waste Athenian money, there were plenty of other desolate headlands to fortify apart from this one. They had heard too that an enemy fleet had already set out for Corcyra and were anxious to engage it as soon as possible.

In the end Demosthenes' plan was carried out almost, as it were, by accident. A storm forced the Athenian fleet to take refuge in the harbour of Pylos and, as the bad weather continued, the soldiers got bored with having nothing to do. Quite suddenly they got the idea of occupying themselves in building fortifications on the part of the headland joining the land. They had no iron tools for shaping the stones, and simply picked them up by hand and arranged them as best they could. Where mortar was required, they carried it on their backs, stooping down so as to carry as much as possible and clasping their hands behind them to prevent it slipping off. Beginning with no very clear idea of what they were doing, they got more and more enthusiastic about their work and in six days had built reasonably good fortifications along the landward side and strengthened some weak places on the sides facing the sea.

At first the Spartans did not take the news of the occupation of Pylos very seriously. They were celebrating a religious festival at the time and they believed that, in any case, as soon as they appeared on the scene, the Athenians would withdraw, or else they would capture the fortifications without difficulty. Also the bulk of their army was still in Attica.

After six days the weather cleared and Eurymedon and

Sophocles hurried on to Corcyra, leaving Demosthenes and five ships as a garrison.

Meanwhile the Spartans in Attica were taking a more serious view of the situation. Their commander, the Spartan King Agis, rightly saw that Pylos in Athenian hands was a very serious threat indeed. The helots under Spartan domination would be encouraged to revolt if they had a safe refuge, and the very idea of an Athenian army occupying Spartan land seemed intolerable. The invasion forces were withdrawn from Attica after only fifteen days and the Peloponnesian fleet of sixty ships was instructed to return from Corcyra. Demosthenes could see that his small force was to be attacked at once by land and sea, and immediately sent out two of his ships to urge Eurymedon to come back with his fleet and bring help.

And now the Spartan fleet, which had managed to avoid making contact with the Athenians, arrived on the scene. They expected that the Athenians would send naval reinforcements and made their plans accordingly. For the time being they had command of the sea and Demosthenes was forced to beach the three ships he had left under the shelter of his fortifications while the Spartans sailed into the harbour of Pylos.

Across the mouth of this harbour lies the narrow island of Sphacteria, providing shelter to the harbour from the open sea. It is about a mile and a half long, is thickly wooded and uninhabited. Two narrow channels separate it from the land. On the north, facing the headland of Pylos and the Athenian fortifications, the channel would leave room for only two ships abreast and on the southern end there would be room for eight or nine. The Spartan plan was to guard these two entrances with lines of ships placed close together with their prows facing the sea and at the same time to land a force of hoplites, or heavy infantry, on Sphacteria, so as to prevent the Athenians landing there. In this way they hoped to avoid having to fight a battle at sea and to blockade the Athenians on land so effectively that they would soon be forced to surrender. They sent their hoplites over to the island and first of all, before the Athenian fleet could arrive, attempted to take the Athenian fortifications by assault.

Demosthenes saw that he would have to meet an attack by land from the north across the neck of the headland and also an attempt at a landing from the sea. He did what he could to meet the situation. He had enrolled a few hoplites from the local population and armed as best he could the sailors from his ships. But he was short of arms and many of these sailors had to be content with shields made of osiers. He posted most of his men, fully armed or not, in the sector facing the land, where the fortifications were strongest. Then he picked out a force of about sixty hoplites and a few archers and with these went outside the wall down to the sea at the point where he thought the enemy would be most likely to attempt a landing. The fortifications here were incomplete, since the Athenians had assumed that their own ships would always be in control of the sea.

Demosthenes encouraged his men by pointing out that, dangerous as their position was, these dangers too could be surmounted. 'In fact,' he said, 'so long as we are determined to hold our ground and do not yield an inch, I consider that the odds are on our side. Do not be afraid of the enemy's numbers. They mean nothing, so long as they are unable to make a landing and make use of them. This is a difficult place for a landing; they can only come in with a few ships at a time, and if we meet them at the water's edge, the advantage will be all with us. You yourselves, unlike the Spartans, have had plenty of experience at landing from ships on enemy territory and you know how difficult an operation it is if the defenders stand firm. This is what you must do: stand firm and you will save your own lives and the fortifications as well.'

These considerations made the Athenians feel more confident. They marched down to the water's edge and prepared to meet the enemy's attack. And now the Spartans made their assault on the position from both land and sea. In the attack from the sea forty-three ships were engaged. They came on in small detachments, relieving each other in turn, so that there was continuous fighting, and they attempted to make their landing just where Demosthenes had expected. On the Spartan side Brasidas, in particular, distinguished himself in the fighting. He was in command of a trireme and when he saw that the other captains and the steersmen were proceeding cautiously because of the difficulties of the rocky coast and because they feared to endanger their ships, he shouted out to them, asking what was the point in sparing ships' timbers and meanwhile tolerating an enemy force on Spartan soil, and telling them to break up their ships so long as they could force their way on shore. He forced his own steersman to run his ship aground and sprang up on the gangway to lead his men ashore. Here the Athenians fell upon him and after he had received many wounds he fell down fainting into the bows of the ship. His shield slipped from his arm into the sea and was later picked up by the Athenians and used for the trophy they put up after the attack.

The others still fought on bravely but could not force a landing, as the Athenians stood firm and did not yield an inch of ground. It was a strange battle altogether and quite contrary to the usual run of things, with Athenians fighting on land—and Spartan land too—against Spartans fighting from ships.

The attacks continued all that day and part of the next day. The assault from the land had been no more successful than that from the sea and finally the Spartans broke off the action and sent away some of their ships to fetch timber for making siege engines.

At this point the Athenian fleet arrived. It had been reinforced on the way and was now fifty ships strong. They saw that the mainland and the island of Sphacteria were thick with enemy hoplites and that the enemy fleet was in the harbour, and they formed line of battle in the open sea, hoping that the Spartans would come out and engage them. The Spartans, on their side, had no intention of sailing out into the open sea where the superior seamanship of the Athenians would give them a great advantage; nor had they blocked the entrances into the harbour, as they had meant to do. They manned their ships and prepared to fight inside the harbour.

Seeing this, the Athenians sailed into the harbour by both entrances and fell upon the Spartan fleet and put it to flight, disabling a number of ships and capturing five. They then turned on the ships that had fled to shore, ramming some of them and attempting to tow off others.

The Spartans were now overwhelmed with horror. They saw that the Athenians were in complete control of the harbour and that their men on the island were cut off. They rushed into the water in full armour, tugging at the ships and trying to save what remained of their fleet. After a bitter struggle, with many wounded on both sides, they succeeded in rescuing the empty ships except for the ones that had been captured first. The action was broken off and the Athenians put up a trophy and gave back the Spartans their dead under a truce. Then they immediately began to cruise round the island where the enemy force was trapped. There were four hundred and twenty regular Spartan soldiers on the island, together with their attendant helots.

The Spartan authorities were now willing to make almost any concession in order to get their men back. They negotiated for an armistice at Pylos and at the same time were ready to send ambassadors to Athens to sue for peace. In the terms for the armistice which were agreed on the Athenians demanded that the Spartans should hand over their entire fleet and should cease all military operations. In return the Athenians would allow rations to be sent in to the men on the island under Athenian supervision and would escort the Spartan representatives to Athens and back again. The armistice should last until the return of the Spartan ambassadors, on which the Spartan ships should be given back. If there was the slightest infringement of these terms by either side, the armistice should be considered null and void.

The Spartans were now willing to do anything for peace. They handed over their ships, about sixty altogether, and their representatives, when they reached Athens, offered the Athenians the lasting friendship and alliance of Sparta. They now no longer claimed that the war had been caused by Athenian tyranny and imperialism, nor did they pretend that Sparta had been fighting for the liberties of Greece. Instead they maintained that no one quite knew how the war had started, and offered Athens all the credit for, if she accepted their proposals, giving back to the Greeks the benefits of peace.

The Spartan delegates in fact made it perfectly plain that Sparta was now prepared to sacrifice the interests of her allies and give Athens all the security that she had been fighting for. And there were many Athenians who would have been glad to make peace on these terms. The majority, however, were inclined to think that, having won so much, they could now win still more. They were encouraged in particular by Cleon, who proposed first that the men on the island should surrender and be brought to Athens, and that then Sparta should give back to Athens strongpoints on the isthmus of Corinth which had once been conquered by Athens but had then been returned to Megara. He also claimed a large part of the northern coast of the Gulf of Corinth, which Athens had once held but had given back to Achaea, a member of the Spartan League. After that, he said, Sparta should recover her men and a peace should be made.

Such terms were, as Cleon knew, humiliating in themselves and impossible for the Spartans to accept openly without making it clear to all the world that Sparta was ready in her own interests to abandon the territory of her allies to Athens. Even so the Spartans declared that they were ready to discuss these proposals, but that they would prefer to discuss them in a small committee and point by point in a calm atmosphere. This was enough to bring Cleon down on them at once. He said that he had always known that their intentions were dishonest and now the fact was proved by their unwillingness to speak in front of the whole people. This, of course, was impossible for the Spartans to do. Moreover they were far from sure that, even if they did accept Cleon's demands and disgrace themselves in front of their allies, they would get the peace they wanted. Cleon was perfectly capable of going on to demand still more humiliating concessions. So they left Athens without having achieved anything.

On their return to Pylos the armistice was at an end and the Spartans asked for their ships back again according to the agreement. The Athenians then alleged that the treaty had been broken. They claimed that there had been an attack on the wall and also brought forward a few other minor complaints. They therefore refused to give the ships back. All the Spartans could do was to deny the Athenian allegations and to make a formal protest against the injustice of the Athenian action. They then prepared to renew the fighting.

Meanwhile twenty more ships had arrived from Athens and the blockade of the island was intensified. By day there were always two ships on patrol, sailing round the island from opposite directions and at night the whole fleet of seventy sail was anchored all round it. The Spartans on their side kept up their attacks on the fortifications separating Pylos from the mainland and did all they could to smuggle in supplies to their men marooned on the island.

11. Athenian Victory at Pylos

THE Athenians had expected to be able to subdue the men on the island, who were under close blockade and had only brackish water to drink, within a few days. However the operation proved much more difficult than had been expected. They themselves were short of water, since all they had came from a small spring on Pylos; they had no port facilities and there were constant difficulties in supplying their large force. And the Spartans were doing everything they could to get food to their men. Helots were promised their freedom if they could carry provisions to the island and large money rewards were offered as well. In bad weather or on dark nights it was often possible to elude the Athenian patrol ships, and the Spartans knew that if their men could only hold out until the winter the Athenians would have to break off the blockade.

All this caused a lot of discouragement at Athens. People now wished that they had accepted the Spartan offer of peace and began to blame Cleon for having led them astray. Cleon himself was alarmed at his growing unpopularity. First he insisted that all the reports coming to Athens were exaggerated. The messengers then told him to go to Pylos himself and see whether they were or not. Knowing that if he did this, he would have to admit that he had been wrong, he said that it was a waste of time to keep on sending inspectors. What they wanted to see was more energy and enterprise from the generals. And, pointing to Nicias, who was general at the time, a moderate man whom he personally detested, he declared that if the generals were real men they would have captured the Spartans on the island already. He added that if he had been in command the whole operation would be over by now.

Nicias retorted that he was perfectly prepared to let Cleon take out a force and do what he said he could do, if he thought it so easy. Cleon was now thoroughly scared and did everything he could to back out from what he had said. The Athenians behaved in the way crowds usually do. The more Cleon tried to back out of the command, the more they insisted that he should sail. Finally, seeing that there was nothing else for it, Cleon boldly declared that he was not frightened of the Spartans and that within twenty days he would either kill them or bring them back alive. This wild claim caused a certain amount of laughter, though the more intelligent people present reflected that, however things went, there would be a solid advantage: either they would see the last of Cleon (which was what they rather expected) or else they would have the Spartans in their power.

Cleon meanwhile was intelligent enough to have Demosthenes appointed as his colleague in the command. In fact he had heard that Demosthenes was already planning an all-out assault on the island and he took out from Athens with him just the troops which Demosthenes needed—light-armed infantry and four hundred archers.

Up to this time Demosthenes had hesitated to attack because of what seemed to him the difficulties of the position. The island was thickly wooded and the defenders, who knew the ground, would have very great advantages. They would be able to concentrate at the few landing-places or ambush his men if they did succeed in landing and tried to move forward. However, an accidental fire had broken out on the island, stripping it of most of its cover. Demosthenes could now see that there were more Spartan troops on shore than he had thought, but he saw too that there were more possible landing-places and that the rough and broken ground in the interior was ideally suited to an attack supported by slingers, archers and light infantry. Under the same sort of conditions he himself had suffered a serious defeat in northern Greece. He now profited by that experience.

As soon as Cleon arrived the two generals sent a message to the Spartans on the mainland asking whether they were prepared, in order to avoid further fighting, to instruct the men on the island to surrender and promising that, if they did so, they would only suffer a mild form of imprisonment and would be released as soon as a general settlement was reached. The Spartans without hesitation refused this offer. At this time it was an unheard-of thing for any Spartan soldier to surrender.

Demosthenes and Cleon waited for one day and then attacked. They embarked all their hoplites in a few ships and landed before dawn on both sides of the island—from the open sea and from the harbour—about eight hundred of them altogether. They then ran forward at once against the first enemy strongpoint. The enemy dispositions were as follows. In this first guard post there were about thirty hoplites; the centre and the most level part of the island, where the water was, was held by the main body under their commander, Epitadas; and at the very end of the island opposite Pylos there was another small detachment guarding an old fort which was built on rocky and steep ground and which they thought would be useful if they were ever forced to retreat.

The Athenian landing took the Spartans by surprise. The first guard post was quickly overrun and the men there, who were still asleep or half-armed, were destroyed. At dawn the rest of the army landed. This consisted of the crews of more than seventy ships, armed as best they could be, eight hundred archers, at least eight hundred light infantry, and all the Athenian and allied troops at Pylos except for those guarding the fortifications. Demosthenes divided this force into companies about two hundred strong, who occupied the highest parts of the ground with the idea of making things difficult for the enemy in whatever direction he might turn. For he would always be attacked from the rear and from both flanks and, as Demosthenes had found, these attacks are very difficult to meet in rough and broken country, since light-armed troops have all the advantages of mobility. They can go on inflicting casualties at long range, can easily fall back if they are attacked and then come on again as soon as the pursuit slackens.

As soon as they saw that their first post had been overwhelmed, Epitadas and the main body of the Spartans advanced against the Athenian hoplites. Meanwhile the light troops swarmed around them on both flanks and from the rear, and the Athenians held their positions without advancing to meet them. So the Spartans were unable to get to close quarters with the hoplites or make any use of their specialised training. They found themselves engaged in a kind of fighting in which they had no experience. Stones, javelins and arrows rained down on them from every side and if they charged in one direction, the enemy easily eluded them there and meanwhile attacked all the more fiercely from the other directions. As the battle went on, the light-armed troops grew more and more confident. At first they had been obsessed with the idea that they were actually going to attack Spartans, but now they were finding that these Spartans were not so terrible after all and they began to despise them, shouting as they charged down on them and letting loose with everything they had. A cloud of dust rose from the burnt ashes of the fire and the Spartans could scarcely see where they were or hear the words of command.

Finally, after many of them had been wounded, they closed their ranks and began to fall back on the fort at the end of the island, which was not far off and was garrisoned by their own men. Seeing them give way, the light-armed troops shouted all the louder and bore down on them with even greater confidence. Those whom they managed to intercept and surround they killed, but the majority of the Spartans reached the shelter of the fort, rejoined their garrison and took up positions along the whole length of the fortifications. The Athenians followed them up and tried to storm the place from the front. But the Spartans now found it easier to defend themselves since they were no longer encircled on their flanks.

Most of the day the fighting went on and both sides held out, tired as they were with their efforts and with the thirst and the sun, and it seemed that the struggle might go on indefinitely. In the end, however, one of the allied commanders approached Cleon and Demosthenes and told them that he could find a route to the high ground in the rear of the enemy. He asked for a force of archers and light troops to go with him and they gave him what he asked for.

With great difficulty he managed to get this force up on to the heights by a route which the Spartans had considered impassable and so left unguarded. These troops, suddenly and unexpectedly appearing in the rear, struck panic into the Spartans, who now found themselves again encircled. They were exhausted from lack of food, and, as the Athenians pressed their attack more confidently, they fell back, leaving the approaches to the fort in Athenian hands.

At this point Cleon and Demosthenes stopped the fighting. They saw that, if it went on, the Spartans would be massacred and they wanted to bring back some of them alive to Athens. So they made a proclamation by a herald, asking them if they would surrender themselves and their arms to the Athenians to be dealt with at their discretion.

Most of the Spartans, hearing the words of the herald, lowered their shields and waved their hands to show that they accepted the terms. Their commander, Epitadas, had been killed and the second-in-command, though still alive, was lying among the dead bodies and was thought to be dead himself. The next senior officer met with Cleon and Demosthenes and asked to be allowed to send to the Spartans on the mainland for instructions. There were two or three exchanges of messages between the men on the island and the Spartan officials on shore. The last message brought over to the island was: 'The Spartans order you to make your own decision about yourselves, so long as you do nothing dishonourable.'

After further discussion among themselves the men on the island surrendered. Out of the four hundred and forty hoplites that had crossed over, two hundred and ninety-two were taken alive to Athens; the rest had been killed. About one hundred and twenty of the prisoners were of the Spartan officer class. Since there had been nothing in the nature of a pitched battle, the Athenian losses were light.

This event caused more surprise in the Greek world than anything else that happened in the war. Up to this time it had been generally believed that Spartans would never surrender under any circumstances, but would keep their arms to the last and die fighting as best they could.

The Athenians, when their prisoners reached Athens, kept them under guard until a settlement should be reached and informed the Spartan government that if they invaded

Attica before then, the men would be taken out and put to death. Meanwhile Pylos remained strongly garrisoned and became a centre for helots who wished to revolt. Bands of these raided the Spartan territory and did much harm, the Spartans being quite unused to this kind of guerilla warfare. They became more and more anxious for peace; but the Athenians turned down all their offers. They still aimed at gaining even more.

12. Athenian Defeat at Delium.
Loss of Amphipolis

SPARTA was now on the defensive. She had lost her whole
fleet and she was afraid to invade Attica by land. The
Athenians made full use of the initiative they had gained.
Nicias, with eighty ships and transports for cavalry,
launched a large sea-borne landing in the territory of
Corinth and defeated the Corinthians in battle. He went on
to ravage parts of the northern Peloponnese and to capture
and fortify another base on the coast, at Methana. Meanwhile another Athenian fleet was operating in Sicily,
demonstrating the extent of Athenian sea power but, apart
from that, not achieving anything important.

Next summer, the eighth of the war, Nicias struck a still

more damaging blow against Sparta by capturing the island of Cythera, which lies off the southern coast of Spartan territory and is the chief port for merchant ships from Egypt or Sicily. With the loss of this island Spartan morale sank still lower. The Spartans now never knew where the Athenians would land next; they were terrified of a general revolt of the helots; and they found themselves fighting the kind of war for which they were entirely unprepared and unequipped. Their large army, trained for pitched battles, was quite useless against these sudden unexpected raids from the sea. They found themselves forced to rely on cavalry and archers and, since this was not at all what they were used to, they showed themselves more and more timid and irresolute in their operations.

Later in this same summer another Athenian army nearly succeeded in capturing Megara and cutting Sparta off from her allies in northern Greece. The Athenians did capture the fortifications running from Megara to the sea and the port of Nisaea, but Megara herself was saved at the last moment by Brasidas. In these operations Athens had been helped by a pro-Athenian democratic party in Megara and now even in Boeotia democrats in the various cities were beginning to make overtures to the Athenian generals. The new policy of aggression in all fields, by land as well as sea, which was by no means the policy recommended by Pericles, appeared to be successful everywhere.

In fact, however, though Athens had gained enormously in prestige and though her naval victories had given her complete control of the seas, her suffering in the war had already been enormous. She had lost about a third of her population in the plague and, apart from this, there had been many casualties, particularly among the hoplites and the cavalry, in the fighting. Also, while the Spartan alliance was certainly showing signs of breaking up, all was far from well in the Athenian alliance. Taxes and tribute money had been increased and this naturally led to unrest, particularly among the richer classes; in the important areas of Thrace and Chalcidice, several cities were ready to revolt; and in Sicily a very able Syracusan statesman had persuaded most of the Sicilian states to make peace among themselves and so leave no pretext for Athenian intervention. The angry mood and the vast ambitions of the Athenian people were shown when their forces returned from Sicily without having accomplished anything. Two of the generals were exiled and a third fined on a charge of bribery. The Athenians, ignorant of the real state of affairs in Sicily, had expected to gain control of the whole island.

Sparta remained ready and, indeed, anxious for peace, and peace would have been welcome, too, to many of the richer and middle classes in Athens, who had lost most in the war. But the mass of the Athenian people, whose spokesman was still Cleon, were opposed to any settlement while there was still more that might be gained. Two events altered this state of affairs; one was the defeat of the Athenian army on land in one of the only pitched battles of the war; the other was the success of Brasidas in undermining the Athenian alliance in the northern Aegean.

The defeat on land took place in the winter following the campaign at Megara. It came after the failure of a plan to gain control of the whole of Boeotia. For its success this plan depended on careful timing and on assistance from pro-Athenian parties in several Boeotian cities. Demosthenes was to land on the south-west coast of Boeotia and on the same day the city of Chaeronea in the north was to be seized by rebels, and the main Athenian army, under its general Hippocrates, was to advance into southern Boeotia, seize the sanctuary of Apollo at Delium and fortify it as a rallying-place for other pro-Athenian forces in the country. However the plot was betrayed to the Boeotian authorities and none of the expected revolts took place. Owing to a mis-understanding Demosthenes arrived too early and, receiving none of the support he had expected, could do nothing but go away again. Meanwhile Hippocrates with the Athenian field army of cavalry, hoplites and light infantry was on his way to Delium. After reaching the place and fortifying it, he sent his light troops back to Athens, left a garrison behind and then with the rest of the army began to march back to Athens himself. By this time the whole forces of Boeotia had mustered and were close to him. Most of the Boeotian generals, seeing that the Athenians were retiring, were in favour of leaving them alone and of concentrating on re-capturing Delium. But the Theban general, Pagondas, persuaded them instead to attack the main Athenian army.

The battle took place late in the day and its result was determined by the tactics and leadership of Pagondas himself. The numbers of cavalry and hoplites on both sides were about equal, but the Athenian light-armed troops were too far on their road back to take part in the battle. Pagondas with his Thebans was on the right of the Boeotian line and he drew his force up in files twenty-five men deep, while the rest of the army and also the whole of the Athenian line was drawn up in files of the usual depth of eight men each. His cavalry and more than ten thousand light-armed troops were on the wings.

Pagondas led the attack with the slope of a hill in his favour and after some hard fighting the superior weight of his massed formation of Thebans broke through the left of the Athenian line. Meanwhile the Athenian right had routed the enemy in front of them and were in hot pursuit, thus losing contact with their own left. Pagondas was able to send out squadrons of cavalry behind the shelter of a hill and charge the victorious Athenians from the rear. This was the beginning of the rout of the whole Athenian army, who now, as they attempted to get back towards Attica, were attacked from all sides by cavalry and light troops. Fortunately for them it was now late in the day so that most of them were saved by the darkness. But Hippocrates and more than a thousand of his best troops had been killed. Later the garrison at Delium was overwhelmed and, though some of it got away by sea, two hundred Athenians were taken prisoner. The Boeotians on their side had lost about five hundred hoplites, but they could afford losses much better than could Athens whose resources in man-power were already strained. The result of this battle showed how correct had been the judgement of Pericles who had advised the Athenians never to risk their whole army in one engagement.

Meanwhile the Spartan Brasidas had been carrying out some brilliant campaigns in the north. He had gone there in response to an appeal for help from Perdiccas, the King of Macedonia, who claimed to be alarmed by Athenian successes in that area and offered help to any Spartan army that would come to encourage revolt against Athens among the subject cities. It was Brasidas who persuaded the Spartan army authorities to let him go. He had only one thousand seven hundred hoplites, most of whom he had raised himself in the Peloponnese, and the Spartans only consented to the expedition because they were alarmed and depressed by constant Athenian attacks on their own territory and by the fear of revolt among their own subjects; they wanted to cause Athens trouble, but gave Brasidas little support and never expected him to achieve what by his own great abilities he did achieve.

His first problem was to make contact with King Perdiccas and in order to do so he had to march through Thessaly, which was on friendly terms with Athens. This would have been impossible if the Thessalians had made anything like a determined effort to stop him. But Brasidas, partly by skilful diplomacy, partly by moving with great speed, got through Thessaly unopposed. As soon as they heard that he had reached Thrace the Athenians declared war on Perdiccas, who had deceived them as he was soon to deceive Brasidas. For Brasidas found that what Perdiccas really wanted was to use him and his army in dealing with enemy tribes in the west who had nothing whatever to do with the war between Athens and Sparta. Brasidas, however, put Perdiccas off for the time being and moved into Chalcidice with the aim of fostering revolt among the cities loyal to Athens.

His success here was due to his own moderate and upright conduct. He told the cities that he came as a liberator and wished nothing except that they should be independent and enjoy whatever system of government they pleased. He was, for a Spartan, an extremely good speaker and he won people over by his eloquence as well as by his sincerity. He was far the most popular and successful of any Spartan officer who was sent abroad in this war. Most of the others showed themselves to be arrogant, tyrannical and narrow-minded.

By the time of the battle of Delium Brasidas had already won over several cities in Chalcidice and his energy and generosity made it likely that he would win over more. His next objective was the very important city of Amphipolis, controlling the passage of the river Strymon and communications with the interior of Thrace. There was a small party in Amphipolis ready to open the gates to Brasidas and his army when he arrived.

In Athens alarm was already felt because of Brasidas' successes, but, as a result of the campaign at Delium, no reinforcements had been sent out to the commanders on the spot. These were Eucles, who was in Amphipolis, and I myself, Thucydides, the author of this history, who was in the island of Thasos, about half a day's sail away, with seven ships.

Brasidas moved rapidly and in snowy weather. Marching all through the night, he reached the outskirts of Amphipolis before anyone except the conspirators knew that he was on his way. The city of Amphipolis is surrounded on two sides by the river Strymon, and Brasidas had forced his way over one of the bridges and was close to the main fortifications before dawn. He captured most of the citizens who were outside the walls and took over all their property. Others managed to flee inside the walls and for some time there was a state of panic inside the city. But those who wanted to betray the city were in a minority and the gates were not opened to Brasidas as he had hoped. The position was a strong one and for the time being Brasidas camped where he was.

Eucles immediately sent a messenger to me in Thasos, asking me to come to his relief. I set out as soon as the message reached me. My first aim was, of course, to save Amphipolis; but if it surrendered before I could arrive I hoped at least to save the port of Eion at the mouth of the Strymon.

Brasidas, meanwhile, knew that he had to act quickly. He expected a naval force to arrive from Thasos and he had heard that I had the right of working the gold-mines in that part of Thrace and because of this had considerable influence with the people in the area. He feared that, if I could arrive in time, the people of Amphipolis, with the support of my ships and prospects of help from the surrounding country, would feel secure. So he made a proclamation offering very moderate terms by which anyone who wished, Athenian or not, could stay in the city with his rights guaranteed, and any who preferred to leave could do so, taking their property with them; the prisoners in Brasidas' hands would be released and their property restored to them. These terms were better than anyone had expected and now the party in favour of Brasidas came forward openly to recommend them. They were helped by the fact that the friends and relatives of many others were already in Brasidas' hands. So the city was surrendered and late in the same day I sailed into the harbour of Eion with my seven ships. As for Amphipolis, it was already lost and Eion would have been lost too before dawn if I had arrived less quickly. As it was, Brasidas made an attempt to take the place, but we succeeded in beating off his attack.

The fall of Amphipolis, coming on top of the defeat at Delium, was a shocking event to the Athenians. They expressed their anger and disappointment in a way that was now becoming normal. I was blamed for not having saved the place and was exiled.

Brasidas meanwhile continued operations throughout the winter. Other cities allied with Athens came over to him and the movement of revolt began to spread rapidly. Those who had been discontented now at last saw a Spartan acting with energy. Also the general moderation and good sense of Brasidas made him trusted and loved. He sent urgently to Sparta for reinforcements, knowing that he now had it in his power to organise a really serious and important movement away from Athens. But the Spartan authorities distrusted him and were by nature averse from fighting anywhere far from home. All they wanted was peace and to get back their own men who had been captured at Sphacteria. So Brasidas received little if any support and was left to do what he could with the forces he had already. So the winter ended and with it the eighth year of the war.

13. The so-called 'Peace of Nicias'

BY now there was a party in favour of peace in Athens as well as in Sparta, and early in the spring an armistice was arranged. This was to last for one year during which efforts were to be made to reach a complete settlement leading to a lasting peace. Until the peace treaty was made each side should keep what it now had, but there were to be no further hostilities.

Two days after the signing of the armistice the town of Scione, on the western promontory of Chalcidice, came over to Brasidas who, at the time, did not know that the armistice was in effect. He had pledged his word to the citizens of Scione and, when the Athenians demanded that the town should be given up to them, he refused. In Athens Cleon carried in the Assembly a motion that the citizens of Scione should be put to death. Brasidas continued his operations and was now threatening the Athenian base at Potidaea. So, while the armistice was in force elsewhere, fighting continued on this front. An Athenian force was sent out under Nicias who recaptured some places and blockaded Scione. Meanwhile Brasidas' ally, Perdiccas of Macedonia, had quarrelled with him and made peace with Athens. Among the Greek cities in Thrace and Chalcidice Brasidas' reputation was as high as ever, but he was now cut off from the south.

Because of the fighting in the north there had been no progress in making peace, and in spring of the next year the armistice came to an end, with the Spartans still willing for peace but with the Athenians determined to get back what they had lost in the north.

Cleon now persuaded the Athenians to send him out with a considerable army and a fleet of thirty ships. He recaptured the town of Torone, one of the first which had gone over to Brasidas, and then, basing himself on Eion, moved forward against Amphipolis. Brasidas waited for him to make some mistake and Cleon obliged him by doing so. His success at Pylos had convinced him that he was more intelligent than he was; he was always vain and inclined to be over-confident. So now he led his men into a position in front of Amphipolis where they were very vulnerable to the attack of an experienced and resolute commander like Brasidas. At the last moment he decided to retreat, but in doing so he marched his men in column past the gates of Amphipolis, exposing their unshielded right side to an enemy charge. What followed was a rout rather than a battle. Some six hundred Athenians were killed and on the Spartan side only seven men, but one of these seven was Brasidas himself. His men brought him back to the city while he was still alive and he lived just long enough to know that his army had been victorious. He was buried in the market place of Amphipolis and the people for the future sacrificed to him as a hero and honoured him by holding games and making annual offerings to him. They gave him the official title of founder of their colony and destroyed everything that could remind them of Hagnon, the Athenian, who had in fact founded the place sixteen years before.

Cleon had been one of the first to run away. He was overtaken by an enemy soldier and killed. The survivors of the Athenian army made their way to Eion and from there sailed back home. Now both sides had good reasons for making peace. At Delium and Amphipolis Athens had suffered heavy losses. She had also seen her empire in the north beginning to disintegrate. Sparta had been aiming at peace ever since the capture of her men, among whom were Spartans of the highest rank, at Sphacteria. She was also in continual fear of a rising of her subject population. And peace was easier to make now when the two men on each side who had been most opposed to it, Cleon and Brasidas, were both dead. Brasidas had wanted to continue the war because of the successes and honour he was winning and because he believed that he was liberating the Greeks; Cleon because he thought that in a time of peace and quiet people would be less ready to tolerate his violence and his arrogance.

Now the two most influential men in the two states were King Pleistoanax in Sparta and Nicias in Athens. Pleistoanax had suffered from his enemies in time of war and looked forward to a period in which old hatreds would be forgotten. Nicias had done better in his military commands than anyone else of his time. So now, while still untouched by misfortune, he wished to rest upon his laurels and to leave behind him the name of one whose services to the state had been successful from start to finish.

Negotiations continued throughout the year and then, after ten years of war, a peace treaty was signed between Athens on the one side and Sparta and her allies on the other. Prisoners on both sides were to be released; Athens was to evacuate Pylos and other fortified positions she held in the Peloponnese; Sparta and her allies were to give back all Athenian territory which they held, including Amphipolis and the towns taken over by Brasidas. These towns were to have their own governments so long as they continued to pay tribute to Athens, though an exception was made of Torone and Scione, which Athens could deal with as she liked.

After the peace treaty was made there were six and a half years during which neither Sparta nor Athens invaded the other's territory. However, it would be a mistake to consider this a period of peace. In fact during the whole of this time hostilities continued and each side did much harm to the other. There was mutual and growing distrust, each side with justice accusing the other of failing to carry out the provisions of the treaty. If, as one should, one puts together the first ten years' war, the six and a half years of uneasy and unreal truce and the rest of the war down to the time of its end, one will find that the whole war lasted for twenty-seven years. Those who like to believe in oracles will find here one solitary example of their having been proved accurate. I myself remember that throughout the war it was being said that it would last thrice nine years. I lived through the whole of it and was at an age to understand what was happening. After my command at Amphipolis I was banished from my country for twenty years and I saw what was happening on both sides, particularly on the Peloponnesian side, because of my exile, and this leisure gave me rather exceptional opportunities for looking into things.

Soon after the making of the treaty Sparta withdrew her troops from Amphipolis and from the northern front, and Athens gave back the prisoners captured on the island. But the Spartans did not give up Amphipolis to Athens, claiming that they had not sufficient influence with the people of the place, and the Boeotians refused to give back an Athenian frontier fortress which they had seized. In fact they would not subscribe to the treaty at all and remained in a state of truce which had to be renewed every ten days. Corinth and Megara also refused to make a lasting treaty with Athens. These states and others in the Spartan alliance felt that Sparta was sacrificing them in her own interest and feared that any genuine alliance between Sparta and Athens, the two strongest powers in Greece, would mean that every other state would be in danger of losing its independence.

The Athenians, seeing that Sparta was unable or unwilling to control her own allies, felt that they had been cheated. Though they had given back the prisoners, they still kept a garrison of their own in Pylos and refused to give the place up until their claims had been satisfied. So for the next two years there was growing mistrust not only between Athens and Sparta but between Sparta and her own allies.

The result of all this was an increase in strength of the war parties both in Athens and Sparta. It seemed to many of the Spartans that their security depended on the friendship of their powerful allies in Boeotia and Corinth much more than on friendly relations with Athens. And in Athens Nicias, respected, successful and upright as he was, began to be blamed for not having obtained more out of the peace. Nicias' most powerful political opponent was now Alcibiades, a man who would have been thought to be too young for politics in any other state except Athens. Alcibiades was brilliant, handsome and intensely ambitious. He came from one of the noblest families in Athens, was related to Pericles and had been brought up as a ward in Pericles' house. He genuinely believed that there could be no reconciliation between Athens and Sparta, though in his general war policy his own personal ambition certainly played a part. He was a very different leader from Cleon and those like him, since he was not interested in flattering anyone and was in himself a man of outstanding intelligence, energy and ability.

It was under the influence of Alcibiades and against the advice of Nicias that, in the twelfth year of the war, Athens formed an alliance with Argos, the most powerful of Sparta's neighbours, which had up to this time been one of the few neutral states in Greece. This alliance, while it strengthened Athens, also served to unite the Spartan alliance and when, after various inconclusive operations, a pitched battle was fought at Mantinea between the armies of Argos, with Athenian support, and of Sparta and her allies, the result was a crushing victory for the Spartans. After the victory the Spartans drove out the democratic party in Argos and installed an oligarchical government favourable to themselves. This happened at the end of the fourteenth year of the war.

Next year the democrats in Argos regained their confidence and drove out the oligarchs. The Spartans had marched out to help their friends, but, when they heard of their defeat, they went back home to celebrate a festival and delayed all action until the democrats in Argos had had time to fortify themselves and appeal once more for help from Athens. So ended the fifteenth year of the war.

14. The Debate at Melos

IN the following summer the Athenians decided to subdue the small island of Melos. This island is not far off the eastern coast of the Peloponnese and was originally colonised by Sparta. The Melians had refused to join the Athenian empire like the other islanders and had at first remained neutral, without helping either side, but afterwards, when the Athenians ravaged their land, they became open enemies of Athens.

The Athenians now sent out an expedition of nearly forty ships with a large army and landed on Melos. Before doing any harm they sent representatives to negotiate. These representatives were invited to speak, not in front of the whole people, but only to a committee of the governing body. The Athenians began by saying that no doubt the motive in preventing them from speaking before the whole people was to prevent the whole people from hearing an argument which was, in fact, unanswerable. However they were perfectly prepared to speak in front of a few, so long as it was clearly understood that the subject under discussion was nothing more nor less than the safety of their country. Such abstractions as justice and neutrality were, they said, beside the point. The Melians should know that, when these matters were discussed by practical people, the standard of justice depends on the power to compel and that in fact the strong do what they have the power to do and the weak accept what they have to accept.

The Melians then suggested that, even on the level of mere self-interest, it was not good for Athens to destroy the principle of fair play and honest dealing. This was a principle which was to the general good of all men in distress, and there might come a time when Athens herself might need its protection.

The Athenians replied that they were perfectly capable of judging themselves where their own interests lay. So the discussion proceeded and among the points raised were the following:

Athenians: What we propose to do is to show you that it is for the good of our own empire that we are here and that it is for the preservation of your city that we shall say what we are going to say. We do not want any trouble in bringing you into our empire, and we want you to be spared both for your own good and for ours.

Melians: And how could it be just as good for us to be

the slaves as for you to be the masters?

Athenians: You, by surrendering, would save your own lives; we, by not destroying you, would be able to profit from you.

Melians: Would you not agree to us being neutral, on friendly terms with both sides, but allies of neither side?

Athenians: No, because it is not so much your hostility that injures us. But if we were on friendly terms with you, our subjects would regard that as a sign of weakness in us.

Melians: Is that your subjects' idea of fair play—that no distinction should be made between people who are quite unconnected with you and people who are mostly your own colonists or else rebels whom you have conquered?

Athenians: So far as right and wrong are concerned they think there is no sense in the distinction you make. We rule the sea and you are islanders, and weaker islanders too than the others. Many of our subjects would be ready to revolt if they could see in us any sign of weakness. So it is important to us that you should not escape. If you did, it would only encourage the others. They are only too willing to take risks already.

Melians: Surely, then, if they are willing to take such risks to gain their freedom, we, who are still free, would be behaving like cowards and weaklings if we failed to face any danger rather than submit to slavery?

Athenians: No, not if you are sensible. This is no fair fight, with honour on one side and shame on the other. It is rather a question of saving your lives and not resisting those who are far too strong for you.

Melians: Yet we know that in war fortune sometimes makes the odds more level than could be expected if one just looked at the difference in numbers of the two sides. And if we surrender, then all our hope is lost at once, whereas, so long as we remain in action, there is still some hope that we may come through.

Athenians: Hope! It is easy to hope. Yet, unless one has something more solid than that to fall back upon, hope will prove to be something very expensive indeed. Those who, relying on hope, risk their all on one cast only find out what it means when they are already ruined. Do not let this happen to you, you who are weak and whose fate depends on a single movement of the scale.

Melians: It is difficult, and you may be sure we know it, for us to oppose your power and fortune, unless the terms be equal. All the same we trust that the gods will give us fortune as good as yours, because we are standing for what is right against what is wrong; and as for our lack of power, we trust that it will be made up for by the help which we shall receive from the Spartans who are bound, if for no other reason, then for honour's sake to help us. Our confidence, therefore, is not so entirely irrational as you think.

Athenians: So far as the gods are concerned, we think we have as much right to their favour as you have. Our aims and our actions are perfectly consistent with the beliefs men hold about the gods and with the principles which govern their own conduct. Our opinion of the gods and our knowledge of men lead us to conclude that it is a general and necessary law of nature to rule wherever one can. This is not a law we made ourselves. We found it already in existence and we shall leave it to exist for ever among those who come after us. We are merely acting in accordance with it, and we know that you, or anybody else with the same power as ours, would be acting in precisely the same way. Therefore, so far as the gods are concerned, we see no reason why we should fear to be at a disadvantage. But as to your views about Sparta and your confidence that she, out of a sense of honour, will come to your aid, we must say that we congratulate you on your simplicity but do not envy you your folly. In matters that concern themselves and their own constitution the Spartans are quite remarkably good; as for their relations with others, that is a long story, but it can be put briefly and clearly by saying that, of all people we know, the Spartans are most conspicuous for believing that what they like doing is honourable and that what suits their interest is just. And this kind of attitude is not going to be of much help to you in your absurd quest for safety at the moment.

Melians: But surely even their own self-interest will make them want to help us. If they were to betray us, their own colonists and their friends, would they not lose the confidence of all their other friends in Greece?

Athenians: You seem to forget that if one follows one's self-interest one wants to be safe, whereas the path of justice and honour involves one in danger. And, where danger is concerned, the Spartans are not, as a rule, very venturesome. You should remember that you are not in yourselves very important to the Spartans and that it is we, not the Spartans, who control the sea. In fact we must say that we are rather shocked to find that, though you said you wanted to discuss how you could preserve yourselves, in all this talk you have said absolutely nothing which could justify a man in thinking that he could be preserved. Everything you have said so far has been concerned with what you hope may happen in the future, though you can see with your own eyes that the forces you have at present are far too small to give you a chance of survival against what we have with us here and now.

And do not be led astray by a false sense of honour—a thing which often brings men to ruin when they are faced with an obvious danger which somehow affects their pride. If you look at things sensibly, you will see that there is nothing disgraceful in giving way to the greatest city in Greece when she is offering you such reasonable terms—alliance on a tribute-paying basis and liberty to enjoy your property. This is the safe rule—to stand up to one's equals, to behave with deference towards one's superiors and to treat one's inferiors with moderation. Think it over again, then, when we have withdrawn from the meeting and keep this point constantly before your minds—that you are discussing the fate of your country, that you have only one country, and that its future for good or ill depends on this one decision which you are going to make.

The Athenians then withdrew from the discussion. The Melians, left to themselves, did not change from the position they had already taken up. Their answer was this:

Melians: Our decision, Athenians, is just the same as it was at first. We are not prepared to give up in a short moment the liberty which we have enjoyed for so long. We put our trust in the fortune which the gods will send and which has saved us up to now, and in the help of men—that is, of the Spartans; and so we shall try to save ourselves. But we invite you to allow us to be friends of yours and enemies of neither side, to make a treaty which shall be agreeable to both you and us, and so to leave our country.

The Melians made this reply, and the Athenians, just as they were breaking off the discussion, said:

Athenians: Well, at any rate, judging from this decision of yours, you seem to us quite unique in your ability to consider the future as something more certain than what is before your eyes, and to see uncertainties as realities, simply because you would like them to be so. As you have staked most on and trusted most in Spartans, luck and hope, so in all these you will find yourselves most completely deluded.

The Athenian representatives then went back to the army and the Athenian generals immediately began hostilities. They built a wall completely round the city of Melos and, when it was finished, left a garrison behind to blockade the place by land and sea. Twice the Melians succeeded in breaking out through the Athenian lines and bringing in supplies, so that they were able to hold out through the summer. Afterwards another force came out from Athens and tightened the siege so that in the end the Melians surrendered unconditionally. The Athenians put to death all the men of military age and sold the women and children as slaves. Melos itself they took over for themselves, later sending out a colony of five hundred men.

15. The Expedition to Sicily Sets Out

IN the same winter the Athenians decided to sail against Sicily with larger forces than ever before and, if possible, to conquer it. Few of them had a correct idea of the size of the island or of the numbers of its inhabitants and they did not realise that they were taking on a war of almost the same size and difficulty as their war against Sparta and her allies.

At first they voted to send out an expedition of sixty ships under the command of three generals, Nicias, who had been almost always successful in his long military career, Lamachus, also an able commander, and Alcibiades who, of the three, was the most enthusiastic for the expedition and who had the most far-reaching aims of conquest.

Soon after the first vote another assembly was held to vote whatever supplies the generals might ask for and to discuss means of getting the ships ready as quickly as possible. Nicias had not wanted to be appointed to the command; his view was that Athens was making a mistake in starting another war before even the present war had been settled and that the whole enterprise of conquering Sicily was much more difficult than anyone thought. Hoping that he might still induce the Athenians to change their minds, he made a speech pointing out that they were even now only beginning to recover from the effects of the plague and the war and that now was the time to rebuild their resources rather than to indulge in unnecessary and dangerous adventures. Even now they had no firm peace with Corinth or Boeotia; many of the cities in the north were still in revolt and others would join them if Athens wasted her strength on a large campaign in Sicily.

After saying much more along these lines he made a personal attack on Alcibiades, the main leader of the war party, of whose extravagant and disorderly life he disapproved and whose ambitions he distrusted. 'No doubt,' he said, 'there is someone sitting here who is delighted at having been chosen for the command and who, entirely for his own selfish reasons, will urge you to make the expedition—and all the more so because he is still too young for his post. He wants to be admired for the horses he keeps, and, because these things are expensive, he hopes to make some profit out of his appointment. I advise you to beware of him and not to give him the chance of endangering the state in order to live a brilliant life of his own. And I am full of alarm when I see this young man's party sitting at his side in the assembly, all ready to support him in whatever he says. I, on my side, call upon the older and more experienced men among you. Do not, like this young man's friends, indulge in hopeless passions for what is not there. Remember that success comes from foresight and that not much is ever gained simply by wishing for it. Our country is now on the verge of the greatest danger she has ever known. Think of her and, while there is still time, cast your votes against this proposal and vote in favour of leaving the Sicilians alone and of allowing them to manage their own affairs as they please. Remember that the duty of a statesman is simply this, to do all the good he can to his country or, in any case, never to do any harm that can be avoided.'

After Nicias had spoken most of the others who came forward to speak were in favour of making the expedition, though a few supported Nicias. The most ardent speaker opposing him was Alcibiades. He had never seen eye to eye with Nicias in politics and he was now angry at the personal attack which had been made on him. More important motives were his desire to hold the command and his hopes that it would be through him that not only Sicily, but Carthage would be conquered—successes which would bring him personally both wealth and honour. For he was always in the public eye and his passion for horse-racing and other extravagances went beyond what his fortune could supply. This, later on, had much to do with the downfall of Athens. For people became frightened of a quality in Alcibiades which was beyond the normal and showed itself in the extravagance and lawlessness of his private life and the spirit in which he acted on all occasions. They thought he was aiming at becoming a dictator and so they turned against him. In fact in public office his conduct of the war was excellent, but his way of life made him objectionable to everyone as a person; so they entrusted their affairs to other hands and before long ruined the city.

Alcibiades now answered the attack that Nicias had made on him and spoke more enthusiastically than ever in favour of the expedition.

'Since,' he said, 'Nicias has made a personal attack on me, let me begin by saying that I have a better right than others to hold the command and that I think I am quite worthy of the position. As for all the talk there is against me, it is about things which bring honour to my family and myself and which do good to Athens as well. There was a time when many of the Greeks thought that our country had been ruined by the war, but when they saw the splendid show that I made in the Olympic games they began to think that Athens was even stronger than she really is. I entered seven chariots for the chariot race (more than any private person has ever done before) and took the first, second and fourth places, and I saw that everything else was arranged in a style worthy of my victory. People may call me foolish because of the magnificence with which I do things, but it is a useful sort of folly when what I do brings honour not only to me but to the city as well. What I know is that all people who are brilliant and prominent make themselves envied and unpopular in their life-times; but with posterity it is quite a different story; then they are thought of, not as disreputable characters, but as great statesmen and great patriots. This is what I aim at myself and because of this my private life comes in for criticism; but the point is whether you have anyone who deals with public affairs better than I do.'

He went on to point out what he had done in the past and to say that, young as he was, his achievement had already been great; and he advised them to make the best use of everything they had—of him while he still had the vigour of his youth and of Nicias while he still had the reputation of being lucky. As for the difficulties which Nicias saw in the conquest of Sicily, Alcibiades made light of them, and as for the opinion that what was needed now was a time for rest and recuperation, he maintained that, on the contrary, it was the genius and distinction of the Athenian people never to rest but always to be in action.

Seeing the enthusiasm with which Alcibiades' speech was received, Nicias made one last effort to persuade his countrymen to put off the expedition. He thought that they might still change their minds if he made an exaggerated estimate of the forces that would be needed, and so he spoke again, insisting that a much larger number both of ships and of men than had originally been voted would be required. But his speech had just the opposite effect to what he had intended. The Athenians became more enthusiastic than ever and more confident even than before. They voted that the generals should have full powers to commission as many ships and call up as many men as they wanted. And so the whole city turned busily to the most active preparations for the campaign.

While these preparations were going on, the citizens woke up one morning to find that all the stone Hermae in the city had had their faces mutilated by being cut about. These Hermae are a national institution, square-cut figures, assumed to bring luck and protection, which stand in front of private homes and in the temples. No one knew who was responsible for this desecration, but the whole affair was taken very seriously and large rewards were offered for information which might lead to the discovery of the criminals. The whole affair was regarded as a bad omen for the expedition, though many took it to be evidence of some plot against the democracy.

In fact no information was forthcoming about the Hermae, but other stories were told about occasions when statues had been defaced by parties of young men who had been enjoying themselves after having had too much to drink, and also of mock celebrations of religious services which had taken place in private houses. Among those mentioned in this connection was Alcibiades, and the stories were eagerly taken up by his enemies and by those who were shocked by the unconventional character of his private life. They were quick to exaggerate the whole thing and to put it about that it was all a plot to overthrow the democracy and that Alcibiades most certainly had a hand in it.

Alcibiades denied all the charges made against him and demanded that he should be put on trial there and then; if found guilty, he should be put to death; if innocent he should take up his command with no suspicions hanging over him. But his enemies were aware that, if the trial were

held before the expedition set sail, Alcibiades would have
the support of the army and would certainly be acquitted.
So they said that he should sail at once, so as not to hold up
the departure of the expedition, and should stand his trial
when the expedition had returned. In fact their plan was to
bring more serious charges against him in his absence and
then to recall him when they thought they had public
opinion on their side. So it was decided that Alcibiades
should sail with the expedition.

By now it was midsummer and everything was ready
for departure. On the appointed day the Athenians who
were serving and all their allies who were in the city went
down to Piraeus at dawn and manned the ships for putting
out to sea. The rest of the people, in fact almost the entire
population of Athens, citizens and foreigners, went down
to Piraeus with them. Those who were natives of the country
all had people to see off, friends, husbands, brothers, sons,
and they came full of hope and full of sadness at the same
time, thinking of the conquests which might be made and
thinking, too, of those whom they might never see again
considering the long voyage on which they were going from
their own country. At this moment when they were really
on the point of parting from each other with all the risks
ahead, the danger of the situation came more home to them
than it had at the time when they had voted for the expedition. Nevertheless they were heartened by the thought of
the strength they had and by the sight of the quantities of
every kind of armament displayed before their eyes. As for
the foreigners and the rest of the crowd, they came merely
to see the show and to admire the incredible ambition of

the thing.

Certainly this expedition that first set sail was by a long way the most costly and the finest-looking force of Hellenic troops that up to that time had ever come from a single city. Apart from the great sums spent on it by the state, there had been a lot of private competition among the captains of the ships and the commanders of the land forces, each one wanting to be conspicuous for the efficiency of the men under his command and for the splendour of their equipment. To an outside onlooker it appeared more like a demonstration of the power and greatness of Athens than an expeditionary force setting out against the enemy. And what made this expedition so famous was not only its astonishing daring and the brilliant show that it made, but also its great preponderance of strength over those against whom it set out, and the fact that this voyage, the longest ever made by an expedition from Athens, was being undertaken with hopes for the future which were enormous and almost unlimited in scope.

When the ships were manned and everything had been taken aboard, silence was commanded by the sound of the trumpet and the customary prayers made before putting to sea were offered up, not by each ship separately, but by all of them together, following the words of a herald. The whole army had wine poured out into bowls, and officers and men made their libations from cups of gold and silver. The crowds on the shore too joined together in the prayers. Then, when the hymn had been sung and the libations finished, they put out to sea, first sailing out in column, and then racing each other as far as the island of Aegina. So they made good speed on their way to Corcyra, where other forces of their allies were mustering to join them.

16. Sicily. Recall of Alcibiades. His Speech at Sparta

MEANWHILE both rumours and reliable news of the expedition had been arriving in Syracuse. These were taken seriously, particularly by the leading statesman there, Hermocrates, who had already done much to foster a united policy among the Greek cities in Sicily by warning them that, if they failed to stand together, they would fall one by one into the power of Athens. But even now political opponents of Hermocrates continued to maintain that the danger was greatly exaggerated and that Hermocrates' real aim was not so much the safety of Sicily but more power for himself. Nevertheless the Syracusans and their allies made ready for war, though not yet with the urgency and unanimity which Hermocrates had recommended.

By now the Athenian fleet had picked up more troops and supplies in Corcyra and had begun the crossing to Italy and Sicily. There were about one hundred and forty warships and about the same number of transports, merchant ships and smaller craft. The first news that the generals received when they reached Rhegium in Italy was disappointing. They were met here by ships of theirs which had gone ahead to the city of Egesta, which had called them in as allies against Syracuse and had promised to supply great sums of money to help in the support of the expedition. It now appeared that this money did not exist.

What had happened was this: when the first Athenian ambassadors went to Egesta the people of the city had taken them to the great temple of Aphrodite at Eryx and shown them all the offerings of gold and silver that were stored there. The leading citizens had then taken it in turn to entertain the Athenians at their private houses, and everywhere they went the Athenians had been amazed to see the quantities of gold and silver plate and drinking vessels and other valuable objects. So, on their return to Athens, they had quite sincerely reported their opinion that Egesta was one of the richest cities in the world. In fact, however, all they had seen at these entertainments were the same objects over and over again. The Egestans had collected all the valuable plate they had and borrowed more from neighbouring cities, and each citizen in turn made use of the common pool while entertaining the Athenians, thus deceiving them entirely about the wealth and resources of their city. Now the truth had come out and it was found that Egesta was in fact a poor city and could only produce a trifling sum for the campaign.

This news was discouraging both to the generals and to the soldiers, though Nicias had never had much confidence in the ability of Egesta to be helpful to them. Equally discouraging was the fact that none of the Greek cities in Italy had shown any willingness to join the Athenian side. When the generals discussed what to do next, each had a different plan. Nicias was in favour of sailing to Egesta, raising there all the money they could and then seeing to it that Egesta was made safe against attacks from its enemies in the nearby city of Selinus. They should then sail round Sicily, making a demonstration of Athenian power and, after accepting the alliance of any city that would come over to them, should return to Athens. It was wrong, he said, at this stage of the war, to waste the resources of the state on any operation that was likely to prove long or costly.

Alcibiades said that it would be disgraceful, after having sailed out with such a force, to return with nothing to show for it. His plan was first of all to engage in active diplomacy and win over the support of as many Greek cities as possible in Sicily and also to make alliances with the tribes living in the interior. Then, knowing who was for and who against them, they would be in a position to move against Syracuse.

Lamachus, on the other hand, was for making an immediate attack on Syracuse. It was now, he said, when the morale of their own troops was at its highest and the Syracusans were still relatively unorganised and unprepared that they had the best chance of success. And an Athenian victory under the walls of Syracuse would help to bring in

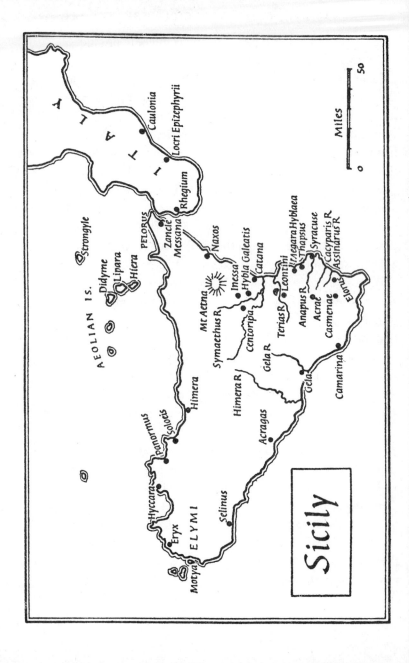

the other cities on their side.

Later events were to show that this plan of Lamachus was, in all probability, the best, but at the time he could convince neither of the other two generals and in the end gave his vote to Alcibiades' plan.

First they manned sixty ships out of their whole force and made a demonstration in front of Syracuse. Sailing into the Great Harbour, where they found no ships manned to meet them, they made a proclamation that they had come to help their allies in Sicily and to give them back everything they had lost at the hands of the Syracusans; and they invited any of their friends in Syracuse to leave the city and join them. At the same time they made a reconnaissance of the approaches and harbours of Syracuse and of places suitable for landing. They then sailed up the coast north of Syracuse, where they had already been received on friendly terms by the people of Naxos, and won over the city of Catana. Here they brought their whole force together and built a camp.

It was while they were at Catana that the state trireme, the *Salaminia*, arrived from Athens with orders to Alcibiades that he was to return to Athens immediately to answer charges made against him with regard to the affair of the Hermae and of sacrilegious conduct. Ever since the expedition had set sail the enemies of Alcibiades had been busy. It became widely believed that the affair of the Hermae was somehow part of a plot to overthrow the democracy and to set up a dictatorship, and Alcibiades, though there was no evidence against him of any kind, was mentioned as being the most likely leader of such a plot. In fact, neither then nor later, did anyone ever discover any certain information about the mutilation of the Hermae, but one of those who had been imprisoned as a suspect was persuaded to come forward, on a guarantee of his own safety, and present a list of people whom he claimed had had something to do with the affair. Among the names on this list were some who had been friends or acquaintances of Alcibiades and, in the general state of public hysteria, suspicion that he was in fact aiming at a dictatorship grew stronger. This suspicion was of course fostered by his enemies, who now thought that if he was brought back to Athens and forced to stand his trial without the support of the army, he would certainly be condemned. However, for fear of causing disturbances in the army in Sicily, they did not venture to order their officers to put Alcibiades under arrest. He was simply instructed to return to Athens in his own ship, escorted by the *Salaminia*.

Alcibiades was perfectly aware how things stood. When, on the way back to Athens, they put in at an Italian port, he and some of his friends left the ship and went into hiding. The crew of the *Salaminia* spent some time in searching for him; then, failing to find any trace of him, returned to Athens without him. Soon afterwards Alcibiades, now an exile, took a ship from Italy to the Peloponnese and arrived in Sparta.

The expeditionary force in Sicily now had only two generals in command, and each of these had opposing policies. Nicias was against taking any undue risks whereas Lamachus was for acting quickly and energetically. And the plan of Alcibiades for winning over other cities and forming a grand alliance against Syracuse was the less likely to succeed, since the skill, energy and diplomatic force of Alcibiades himself were now no longer at their disposal. For the rest of the year, though they made some progress in enlisting support from the tribes of the interior, they failed to win over any important Greek city.

They still, however, retained the initiative and at the beginning of the winter fought a pitched battle outside the walls of Syracuse. In this battle the Athenians and their allies were victorious, but shortage of cavalry prevented them from exploiting their victory to the full and inflicting heavier losses on the enemy and it was too late in the year to begin regular siege operations. So for the rest of the year they returned to their bases at Naxos and Catana and sent to Athens for more cavalry and more money.

The Syracusans on their side spent the winter in training more hoplites, in tightening their military organisation and in strengthening their defences. They also sent ambassadors to the Peloponnese to ask for help. This was promised immediately by Corinth, and some Corinthian ambassadors accompanied the Syracusans to Sparta and joined them in urging the Spartans to action. But their most powerful helper turned out to be Alcibiades who was now in Sparta, exiled from Athens and eager to return there even as a collaborator with his country's enemies.

Alcibiades knew that in speaking to the Spartan Assembly he would have to face considerable prejudice against him. He had done Sparta much harm in the past and he, like Pericles and other members of his family, had been a leader of the Athenian democracy which had always been opposed to Sparta. With regard to the second of these points—his leadership of the democracy—he had this to say: 'My family has always been opposed to dictators; democracy is the name given to any force that opposes absolute power; and so we have continued to act as leaders of the common people. Besides, since democracy was the form of government in Athens, it was necessary for us in most ways to conform to the conditions that prevailed. However, when there was a state of political indiscipline, we always tried to bring the masses back to reason. It is people of this indisciplined sort who have now banished me. But we were leaders of the State as a whole, and our principles were that we should all join together in preserving the form of government that had been handed down to us and under which the city was most great and most free. As for democracy, those of us with any sense knew what that meant, and I just as much as any. Indeed I am well-equipped to make an attack on it; but nothing new can be said of a system which is generally recognised as absurd. But as for changing the system, that seemed to us unsafe while you were engaged in war with us.'

Alcibiades went on to say that the Spartans would be making an enormous mistake if they imagined that the Athenian adventure in Sicily had nothing to do with Sparta. He told them that what Athens aimed at was nothing less than an empire over the whole Mediterranean. After conquering Sicily the Athenians would subdue Carthage and the Greek cities of Italy and the West. Then, with immense resources in men and material, they would turn to Sparta and the Peloponnese. So that it was the future of Sparta herself which was now being decided in Sicily. It was there-fore of the utmost urgency that help should be sent to

Syracuse at once. The Syracusans were under blockade from the sea and had already been once defeated on land. Once Syracuse fell, the rest of Sicily would come over to Athens immediately and from Sicily to Carthage and Italy it was a short step. He therefore advised that two things should be done immediately. First, aid should be sent to Syracuse and in particular a regular Spartan officer should be sent out to take command. And secondly Attica should be invaded again and this time the Spartans should fortify a position in Attica and keep it garrisoned throughout the year. This position should be at Decelea, not far from Athens and a place from which it would be possible to cut Athens off from supplies reaching her by land. This particular move, the fortification of Decelea, was, he told them, just the thing that the Athenians had been fearing for years.

Finally he defended himself against the possible charge that he, who had always been so loyal and patriotic an Athenian, was now turning traitor and joining with his country's enemies. On this point he said: 'The worst enemies of Athens are not those who, like you, have only harmed her in war, but those who have forced her friends to turn against her. The Athens I love is not the one which is wronging me now, but the Athens in which I used to enjoy my rights as a citizen. The country that I am attacking does not seem to be mine any longer; it is rather that I am trying to get back again a country that I have lost. And the man who really loves his country is not the one who refuses to attack it when he has been unjustly driven out of it, but the man whose desire for it is so strong that he will shrink from nothing in his efforts to get back there again.'

This speech of Alcibiades had the effect which he intended, particularly as there were many in Sparta who were already in favour of marching again against Athens. So they decided at once to take steps about fortifying Decelea and to send help to Syracuse. They appointed Gylippus, an able and energetic Spartan officer, to take command of the Syracusans, and Gylippus asked the Corinthians to send him two ships at once and to equip all the other ships they could send so as to be ready by early spring.

While these preparations were going on the winter ended and with it the seventeenth year of the war.

17. Arrival of Gylippus.
Athenian Difficulties

EARLY in the next year the cavalry reinforcements and money which they had asked for arrived from Athens, and Nicias and Lamachus began their siege operations against Syracuse. Their plan was to cut the city off from all reinforcements and supplies both by land and sea, and to do this it was necessary to build long walls extending from the Great Harbour to the south as far as the coast north of the city. The ground near the Great Harbour was low and marshy, but to the north and west of Syracuse there were rocky heights. This area was known as Epipolae, and it was essential to gain control of these heights before operations could be carried further.

At first everything went well for the Athenians. The Syracusan general, Hermocrates, had of course, realised the importance of Epipolae, but he was caught unawares by a surprise landing of the whole Athenian army to the west of the position. After overwhelming Syracusan resistance and counter-attacks, the Athenians built a circular fort on the heights overlooking Syracuse and proceeded to construct from there two walls—one northward to the coast and the other southward to the shore of the Great Harbour.

The Syracusans began at once to build a counter-wall through the level ground at right angles to the southern Athenian wall; they had plenty of workers available in the city and also a certain advantage in time, since the Athenians had first of all to fortify their position on Epipolae. However as soon as the Athenians had done this they sent out a picked force of three hundred men who in a sudden attack captured and destroyed the Syracusan counter-wall. The Syracusans then began to run out another counter-wall consisting of a palisade and a ditch still further south. The Athenians came down at dawn from Epipolae and attacked this wall too, making their way over the marsh by means of doors and planks which they put down to bridge over the worst ground. Soon after daybreak they had captured the ditch and the whole stockade except for a small part which they captured later. By now large forces of Syracusan cavalry and infantry had come up and general fighting broke out. In this fighting the Athenians were victorious, but not before a few of their men, including their general Lamachus, had been killed. The Syracusans were driven back into their city, but, seeing that almost the whole Athenian army was in the plain, they sent out a body of troops to attack the Athenian fort on Epipolae, expecting to find it undefended. And in fact there was no one in the fort except Nicias, who was suffering from illness, and a very few men. The fort itself was saved by the resource of Nicias who, with too few men to beat back an attack, ordered the servants to set fire to the timber and other siege equipment outside the wall. The fire stopped the Syracusans for the critical moments, and before long the Athenians in the plain hurried up to relieve the position. At about the same time the whole Athenian fleet, which had been sailing round from the north, was seen entering the Great Harbour. The Syracusans withdrew from the heights and, seeing all this, began to think that now they had no chance of preventing the Athenians from building their wall down to the sea.

In fact it seemed to many people that the war in Sicily was as good as over. Tribes and cities in the interior which had been waiting to see how things went now openly allied themselves with the Athenians, who also received three fifty-oared ships from the Etruscans. And in Syracuse itself there was general talk of surrender, and many of the Syracusan leaders began to approach Nicias to ask what terms he would give them. The city was now blockaded firmly to the south and the northern blockading wall had almost reached the sea.

By this time the Spartan Gylippus and his ships from Corinth were off the west coast of Greece and anxious to come to the help of Syracuse as soon as possible. But the news that reached them was most alarming; everything seemed to support the untrue story that the Athenian walls

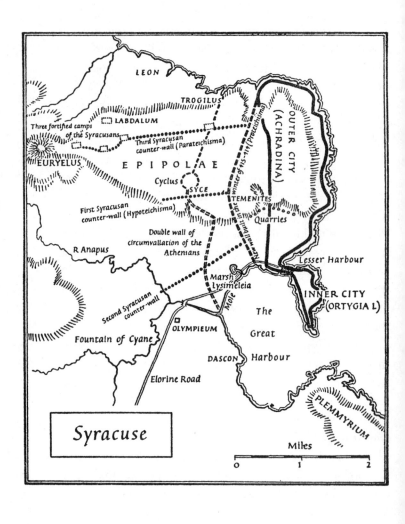

Syracuse

now stretched from sea to sea and that Syracuse was completely blockaded. So Gylippus gave up all hope for Sicily
and decided to try at least to save Italy from the Athenians.
It was not till he reached southern Italy that he received
more reliable news and discovered that the northern Athenian wall was not yet finished and that it was still possible to
get an army into Syracuse by land. He sailed for Sicily at
once with his small fleet and got through the straits of
Messina before the ships which Nicias had sent to intercept
him could arrive. Then, sailing along the north coast of
Sicily he landed at the friendly city of Himera and began to
raise an army. He had seven hundred of his own sailors and
marines and soon more than trebled this force with con-
tingents from Sicilian cities and native tribes who were either
loyal to Syracuse or impressed by the appearance on the
scene of a Spartan commander with Spartan troops. With
his combined forces he set out for Syracuse.

At the same time a Corinthian fleet was on the way to
Syracuse and one of its commanders, Gongylus by name,
reached the city with one ship, ahead of the rest. He found
the Syracusans already discussing how they could make
terms with the Athenians. So close were they to surrender;
but Gongylus encouraged them to hold on by telling them
that a Spartan army was already in Sicily, that more
Corinthian and allied ships were on their way and that Sparta
and her allies would soon be carrying the war into Attica.

Directly after this Gylippus and his army ascended
Epipolae by the same route which the Athenians had taken
and got through the unfinished part of the Athenian wall so
as to join forces with the Syracusans. His coming was the

beginning of an entire change in the situation. Instead of waiting to be completely encircled, the Syracusans began to do everything they could to prevent the completion of the northern Athenian wall. Though Gylippus suffered a defeat in his first effort to drive the Athenians from their positions, he quickly came back to the attack and under the protection of large cavalry forces began to build a cross-wall from the northern fortifications of Syracuse which was intended to cut the Athenian wall before it reached the sea. In the end and after more fighting he was successful. The Syracusan cross-wall was carried past the end of the Athenian fortifications, so that now, even if they won a victory, it was no longer possible for the Athenians to cut Syracuse off from supplies and reinforcements brought in by land.

Nicias now moved his main base from the north of Syracuse to a fortified position at the entrance to the Great Harbour. Here there is a place called Plemmyrium, a headland jutting out into the sea and making the entrance to the harbour a narrow one. Nicias built three forts on this headland and stored most of the equipment inside them, and the larger merchant vessels and fighting ships now made this their station. The position, just opposite the city of Syracuse at the other side of the harbour entrance, had certain advantages but also many disadvantages. Water was in short supply and was not available near at hand, and when the sailors went out to collect fuel, casualties were always occurring because of the Syracusan cavalry. In fact this move to Plemmyrium was the beginning of and chief reason for a general deterioration in the morale of the fleet.

Meanwhile the Syracusans grew more and more confident. They had received considerable naval reinforcements from Corinth and other allies. These ships had managed to elude the ships that Nicias had sent to intercept them and now the Syracusans began to train their crews and prepare to challenge Athens on the sea also, while Gylippus went away into other parts of Sicily to raise still more military and naval forces, and more ambassadors were sent to Sparta and Corinth to press for further support.

Nicias himself was perfectly aware of how serious his position was and, seeing that every day which passed brought new strength to the enemy and increased his own difficulties, he sent an urgent dispatch to Athens. He was convinced that unless the home Government acted immediately and either recalled the expedition altogether or sent out very considerable reinforcements, it could not possibly succeed. Nicias's letter reached Athens in the winter and was read to the Assembly. Though he knew well enough how the Athenians hated to receive bad news, Nicias gave a full and accurate description of the situation. He pointed out that, since the arrival of Gylippus and the reinforcements, the enemy were now in superior numbers and had taken the initiative. There was no longer any possibility of being able to blockade Syracuse unless the Athenians could raise a force large enough to attack and capture the Syracusan counter-wall and, as it was, the Athenian man-power was only barely sufficient to guard its own supply lines. 'The position,' he wrote, 'is that we, who thought we were the besiegers, have become in fact the besieged, at least on land. The enemy are expecting large reinforcements and their plan is, so far as I can see, to attack our fortifications with

their infantry and at the same time to engage us also by sea
with their fleet. And none of you must think it strange that
I use the words "also by sea". The fact is, as the Syracusans
know well, that our fleet was originally in first-class condition; the timbers were sound and the crews in good shape.
But now the ships have been at sea so long that the timbers
have rotted and the crews are no longer what they were. The
enemy has almost unlimited resources of man-power, but
we have to do with what we have and are already fully
extended, what with keeping up the blockade and ensuring
our own supplies. And now many of our slaves and the
foreigners serving with us are deserting us. The whole of
Sicily is united against us; a fresh army is expected from the
Peloponnese, while our troops on the spot are not sufficient
to deal even with the opposition we have at present.

'The time has come for you to decide either to recall us,
or else to send out another force, both naval and military,
as big as the first, and also to send out someone to relieve me
of the command, as I am suffering from a disease of the
kidneys which has made me unfit for service. I think I can
claim some consideration from you, since, in the time when I
had my health, I did you much good service in the various
commands which I held. Finally, whatever you decide to
do should be done quickly, at the very beginning of spring.'

After hearing this letter the Athenians refused to relieve
Nicias of the command and merely appointed two of the
officers in Sicily to share some of the responsibilities with
him. They then voted to send out another military and
naval force, almost as big as the first, under the command of
the generals Eurymedon and Demosthenes. Eurymedon with

the ships and a large sum of money was sent out at once to inform the forces in Sicily that help was on the way. Demosthenes stayed behind to organise the expedition. He was to sail at the very beginning of spring.

The Athenians decided upon this immensely ambitious course at a time when their resources were already strained and when the Spartans were preparing to invade Attica again and to follow the advice of Alcibiades by building a permanent fortress just outside Athens at Decelea. During the winter which ended the eighteenth year of the war, both sides were busy with their plans for greatly extended operations.

18. Athenian Defeats.
Arrival of Demosthenes

AT the very beginning of the next spring the Spartans and
their allies, under the command of King Agis, the son of
Archidamus, invaded Attica and, after laying waste the
countryside, began to fortify Decelea. The fort they built
was about thirteen miles from Athens and controlled the
plain and the richest part of the country.

At the same time large forces from Sparta, Corinth and
other allied states set out for Syracuse. Gylippus also, who
had been raising troops from other cities in Sicily, now came
back to Syracuse with a large army. By this time he felt
secure on land and, supported by the Syracusan general
Hermocrates, he urged the Syracusans to attack the Athen-

ians on the sea also. Up to this time Athenian naval supremacy had been unquestioned, but Gylippus pointed out that
the very fact that Syracusans dared to stand up to the
Athenian navy at all would have a disturbing effect on the
Athenian crews, and he planned to combine the naval attack
on the Great Harbour with a land attack on the forts on
Plemmyrium.

So the Syracusans manned their ships. They had thirty-
five triremes in the Great Harbour behind their defences on
shore and another forty-five in the smaller harbour to the
north of the city. These were to break into the Great Harbour
at the same time as the thirty-five ships already there went
into action. The Athenians on their side manned sixty ships.
With twenty-five of them they fought the thirty-five Syracusan ships in the Great Harbour and sent out the rest to meet
the other attack on the harbour mouth. Here for some time
the fighting was stubborn, with neither side giving way.
Meanwhile the Athenian troops in Plemmyrium had gone
down to the sea and were watching how the battle went. The
result was that they were taken off their guard by the attack
launched by Gylippus on land. Gylippus quickly captured
the largest of the three forts and then the other two as well.
Most of the men inside got safely away to the Athenian
camp, but they left much of their equipment and supplies in
the hands of the enemy. More important still, the Syracusans now had bases at both sides of the entrance to the Great
Harbour. It therefore became much easier for them to
intercept Athenian convoys and supplies.

As for the naval battle, in the end the Syracusans at the
harbour mouth succeeded in breaking into the harbour, but

once inside they fell into disorder and presented the victory to the Athenians, who sank eleven of their ships for the loss of only three of their own. Yet on the balance of the day's fighting the advantage had been with the Syracusans. They had been completely successful on land and, though their lack of experience had cost them the battle on sea, they had still fought well against an Athenian fleet and would be more confident in future.

Meanwhile at home the Athenians were beginning to feel the effects of the enemy occupation of Decelea. In fact this permanent post established in their own country was to do them more and more harm as the years went by and was one of the chief reasons for the decline of their power. The previous invasions had not lasted long and after the invaders had retired the Athenians had been left in full possession of their land. But now they were always deprived of the use of their country and the enemy were on top of them the whole time. In the past they used to import food and supplies from Euboea by the direct overland route, but now everything had to be carried by sea round Cape Sunium and then on to Piraeus. Athens herself, with her long lines of fortifications, had to be guarded day and night so that the place was more like a fortress than a city. So, summer and winter, there was no end to their hardships. What wore them down more than anything else was the fact that they had two wars on their hands at once. Indeed, their obstinate resolution would have seemed impossible to imagine if it had not actually happened. It was incredible that, after eighteen years of war, when Athens herself was besieged, the Athenians should not only not withdraw from Sicily, but actually stay on there and lay siege to Syracuse, a city which was in itself as big as Athens, and should give to the whole Greek world such an astonishing demonstration of their power and of their daring.

Already Demosthenes had organised the second expeditionary force and was on his way to Sicily, first sailing round the Peloponnese and ravaging the country as he went.

After he had set sail there occurred an episode which, while it had no effect on the general conduct of the war, was pitiable in itself and characteristic of the savagery which war brings and which increases while war lasts. In the early summer some one thousand three hundred Thracian mercenaries arrived in Athens just after Demosthenes had set sail. Since they had arrived too late to sail with him they were sent back by sea to their own country under an Athenian officer, who was instructed to use them in raids on the country of Boeotia on the way. Among the places he attacked was the small town of Mycalessus. The Thracians burst into the place at dawn and captured it easily, since no one had expected an attack. They sacked the houses and temples and butchered the inhabitants, sparing neither young nor old, but methodically killing everyone they met, women and children alike, and even the farm animals and every living thing they saw. For the Thracian race, like all the most bloodthirsty barbarians, are always particularly bloodthirsty when everything is going their own way. Among other things, they broke into a boys' school, the largest in the place, into which the children had just entered, and killed every one of them. So disaster fell upon the entire city, a disaster more complete than any, more sudden and more horrible. It was a small city, but its people suffered calamities as pitiable as any which took place during the war.

In Sicily, when it became known that Demosthenes was on his way out with a large relief force, the Syracusans felt it all the more urgent to attack the Athenians again by land and sea. What they had most to fear at sea was the superior skill and seamanship of the Athenian crews; but now, after the capture of Plemmyrium, the Athenians would have much less sea-room in which to carry out the complicated tactics in which they excelled. The battle would be confined to the Great Harbour, in which there would be a lot of ships in a comparatively small space, and the shores of the harbour were for the most part in Syracusan hands, so that the Athenians could only safely back water in the direction of that part of the shore where their own camp was. The Syracusans had also made changes in the equipment of their ships. They had cut down the length of their prows to make them more solid and put extra material into the sides, so as to strengthen them against ramming. They thought that in an enclosed space these heavy, stout and somewhat cumbersome ships, sailing in close formation, would be a match for the faster, lighter Athenian ships.

When they had made these plans they first launched an attack by land and then sailed out with eighty ships against the Athenians, who put out against them with seventy-five ships. In this day's fighting each side was trying out the other's strength and neither side gained any advantage. Two days later the Syracusans attacked again and, after more indecisive fighting, broke off the action at midday. The Athenians thought that the enemy had retired defeated and set about getting their midday meal in a leisurely way. But the Syracusans had had their food already prepared for them on the shore and directly they had eaten they bore down on the Athenians again. The Athenians, most of whom had not yet eaten, hurriedly manned their ships. They had not expected to have to fight again and they sailed out in some confusion, attacking recklessly, since they wanted to get the fighting over. The Syracusans met them prow to prow and with the heavy beaks of their ships stove in the bows of many of the Athenian ships. Javelin-throwers on their decks also did a lot of damage and in the end the Athenians turned and fled to the shelter of their anchorage, pursued closely by the Syracusans, who sunk seven ships and disabled many others.

This victory filled the Syracusans with confidence and it was correspondingly disheartening to the Athenians, who were used to being always victorious at sea. But now, just when the Syracusans were getting ready to make another attack by land and sea, there arrived from Athens another great fleet and another army. Demosthenes sailed into the harbour with about seventy-five ships, about five thousand hoplites and great forces of javelin-throwers, slingers and archers, together with everything else that could be required. This was a moment when the Syracusans and their allies felt real dismay; they thought that their dangers and difficulties would never end, when they saw that, in spite of the fortification of Decelea, another army almost as big as the first one had come out against them and that in every direction the power of Athens was showing itself so great.

Demosthenes saw how things were and realised that it

was impossible for him to let matters drift, as Nicias had done. If Nicias had gone straight to the attack at the beginning, the war might well have been over by now. As it was, his delay had enabled Gylippus to arrive and organise resistance just in time to prevent the completion of the wall which would have shut off Syracuse from any help. Bearing all this in mind, Demosthenes decided that the only way of succeeding was to reoccupy the position on Epipolae, to capture the Syracusan counter-wall and complete the blockade of the city. And now, he thought, while the Athenians were once more superior both on land and sea, was the time to do it. If the operation was successful, Syracuse would be doomed; if it was unsuccessful, they should withdraw at once and not throw away Athenian resources on a hopeless undertaking.

Reconnaissance showed that it would be impossible to make the steep ascent to Epipolae by day without being observed; to capture the position, surprise was essential. So, leaving Nicias and a small garrison to guard the Athenian fortifications, Demosthenes set off about midnight with the rest of the army, taking provisions for five days and all the equipment that would be necessary, if they were successful, for fortifying the heights.

They came up to Epipolae by the same route as that by which the first army had ascended. At first everything went well. They quickly seized the first of the Syracusan forts and pressed on towards the three enemy camps on the high ground. The first Syracusan counter-attack was routed by Demosthenes and the Athenians who immediately pressed on, while others were occupying the Syracusan counter-wall and meeting no serious resistance. Now Gylippus with forces of Syracusans and allies joined the battle, but the daring of this attack by night was something they had not expected; their charge lacked resolution and they were at first forced back on the retreat. The Athenians went on forward, but were now beginning to lose cohesion. They thought the victory was theirs and wanted to cut right through the enemy army so that there should be no chance of their reforming and rallying against them. The first to stand up to them were the Syracusan allies from Boeotia who charged the Athenians, routed their advanced troops and drove them back on the others.

From this moment the Athenians fell into great disorder and did not know where to turn. In fact it was difficult to find out from either side exactly how things happened. In daylight those who take part in an action have a clearer idea of it, though even they cannot see everything, and in fact no one knows much more than what is going on round himself. But in a battle by night (and this was the only one that took place between large armies during this war) how could anyone be sure of what happened exactly? There was a bright moon, but visibility was only what might be expected by moonlight; they could see the outlines of figures in front of them, but could not be sure whether these belonged to their own side or not. Some of the Athenians were being driven back, while others were advancing and others still on the way up and, in the general confusion, not knowing in which direction to march. Then among the Athenian allies the troops from Argos and Corcyra were shouting to each other in their Dorian dialect, so that the Athenians often took them for enemies and in the general confusion, the poor visibility and the uproar of different voices, many parts of the army ended by falling upon each other, friend against friend and citizen against citizen. The panic led to a general rout and, since the way down from the heights was a narrow one, many men lost their lives by throwing themselves down from the cliffs. Most of those who got down safely managed to get back to the camp, but there were numbers, particularly of the troops who had just arrived and who did not know the ground, who lost their way. When day came they were rounded up and killed by the Syracusan cavalry. Many also had thrown away their arms during the flight, so that the quantity of arms captured was out of proportion to the numbers of the dead.

The operation had been close to success, but it had failed, and the Athenian generals now discussed the situation in the light of the defeat. They saw that the soldiers hated the idea of staying on. Many of them were ill, partly because this was the time of the year when there is most illness and partly because the camp was in marshy and unhealthy ground; also the whole future looked desperate. Demosthenes, now that their original plan had failed, was in favour of going away at once, while they still had naval supremacy. The expedition would be far better used, he said, in defending Athens at home rather than against the Syracusans who could no longer be conquered easily.

Nicias agreed that their affairs were in a bad way but he was still reluctant to take the advice of Demosthenes. He believed that the Syracusans were short of money and even now might be forced to give in; and he was in touch with a

pro-Athenian party in Syracuse which kept sending mes
sages to him, urging him not to give up the siege. Also he
thought that in Athens people would never approve of a
withdrawal. Knowing the Athenian character, he felt sure
that even the soldiers who were now clamouring to go home
would, as soon as they got there, entirely change their tune
and say that the generals had been bribed to betray them
and return. And, after his long and honourable career, he
would prefer, he said, to meet his death, if it must be, at the
hands of the enemy rather than be put to death on a disgraceful charge and by an unjust verdict from his own
countrymen. So he voted to stay where they were and go on
with the siege.

Demosthenes was entirely opposed to this. If, he said,
they had to stay in Sicily, at least let them move from
Syracuse to some other base where they would find supplies
easily and where they would be able to use their superior
naval experience in the open sea and not be forced to fight
in a confined space where the advantage was all on the side
of the enemy. And the other general, Eurymedon, supported Demosthenes in this. Nicias, however, continued to
oppose the idea and in the whole business a kind of lack of
resolution began to appear. So the Athenians delayed and
continued to stay where they were.

19. Final Defeat of the Athenian Fleet

MEANWHILE the Syracusans had recovered all the confidence they had lost when Demosthenes and the second expedition had suddenly appeared. The failure of the attack on Epipolae, though it had so nearly succeeded, made them feel that they were invincible and filled them with the highest hopes for the future. By now still more reinforcements were coming to them from the Peloponnese, and Gylippus had gone once more into the interior and come back again to Syracuse with yet another large army.

The Athenian generals could see that their own position, so far from improving, was getting worse every day, particularly because of the sickness that was spreading among their soldiers. They now regretted that they had not moved earlier and even Nicias was prepared to agree that a move was necessary. So orders were given as secretly as possible for everyone to be ready to sail out from the camp when the signal was given. But when they were on the point of sailing, there was an eclipse of the moon, which was at the full. Most of the Athenians took this so seriously that they now urged the generals to wait and Nicias himself, who was of a rather superstitious nature, said that he would not even discuss the question of a move until they had waited for the thrice nine days, which was the period prescribed by the soothsayers. So the Athenians, delayed by the eclipse, stayed on afterwards.

The Syracusans had heard of the Athenian plan to retire and they became more determined than ever not to relax their pressure and to force the enemy to fight again in the confined space of the harbour. So after giving their crews a further period of training they put out against the Athenians with seventy-six ships and at the same time attacked the Athenian fortifications with their ground forces. The Athenians put out against them with eighty-six ships, and Eurymedon, leading the right wing, sailed out from the main body with the idea of encircling the enemy. But the Syracusans first drove back the Athenian centre and then caught Eurymedon in a part of the harbour where there is a narrow bay and where he had no room to manoeuvre. Eurymedon was killed and the ships with him were destroyed. They then drove back the whole Athenian fleet and forced the ships ashore. In the end the Athenian army managed to save most of the ships, but eighteen had been captured by the Syracusans and all the men aboard them killed.

This was indeed a great victory for the Syracusans and it had been won at sea where until now they had been afraid of the naval reinforcements which had come with Demosthenes. The Athenians were now utterly disheartened; they could scarcely believe that this had happened and they wished all the more that the expedition had never been made. Nothing that they had attempted had gone right, and now, after this wholly unexpected defeat at sea, they were at their wits' end.

The Syracusans now began to sail about the harbour without fear of attack and they planned to block up the mouth, so that the Athenians would not be able to slip away, even if they wanted to. From being in a state near despair they had become confident of winning the great glory of defeating the strongest power in Greece and finishing a war which Sparta and the other powers of the mainland had found too difficult for them. For it seemed to them incredible that if the Athenians lost their forces in Sicily they would be able to hold out any longer in Athens or elsewhere. So they began at once to block up the mouth of the Great Harbour, which is nearly a mile wide, with a line of triremes broadside on and merchant ships and other craft at anchor.

When the Athenians saw the harbour being closed and realised what the enemy's plan was, they called a council of war at which it was decided that they would man every ship they had, putting on board every man in the army who could be used, and so fight it out at sea. If they were successful they would sail to another base in Sicily, and if not, they would burn their ships and march away by land.

They carried out this plan at once; first they reduced the area of their fortifications, only manning the defences round their camp and made everyone go on board who was likely to be of service in the coming battle. Altogether they manned about one hundred and ten ships and put aboard them numbers of hoplites, archers and slingers. They strengthened the ships' prows, in the Syracusan manner, and equipped the ships with grappling-irons, since the fighting ahead of them would be close fighting, in fact more like a battle on land than on sea.

And when nearly everything was ready, Nicias, seeing that the soldiers were out of heart because of having been defeated so thoroughly and unexpectedly at sea, called them all together and first gave them some words of encouragement. 'Soldiers of the Athenians and the allies,' he said, 'in the battle ahead each one of us, just as much as the enemy, will be fighting for his life and for his country, since, if we win, each man can see again his native city, wherever it may be. But we must not be downhearted or behave like people with no experience, who, if they lose the first battles, are frightened ever afterwards. On the contrary, you Athenians here and you allies of ours have already had experience of many wars and we must remember that there is always an unpredictable element in warfare and that while we have the courage and the skill to win, the time has come for us to have the good fortune too.

'This time we have done everything possible to help us against the massed formation of enemy ships which must be expected in this narrow harbour. We have altered the construction of our ships and we have equipped them for hand-to-hand fighting, as in a battle on land. It is up to each one of us now to do his part, to drive straight ahead and fight our way into the open sea. You must look down on Corinthians, whom you have beaten so often, and on Sicilians, none of whom even thought of standing up to us when our navy was at its best, and you must drive them back and show that even in sickness and disaster your skill is worth more than the force and fortune of anyone else.

'As for the Athenians among you, I must remind you of this also: you have no more ships like these left in your dock-yards and no reserve of men to fight as hoplites; if this action should end in anything except victory for you, our enemies here will sail against Athens and combine in overwhelming force with our enemies who are there already. So since the fate both of yourselves and of your fellow countrymen at home rests on this one battle, now, if ever, is the time to stand out firm and to remember, each and all, that those of you who are going aboard the ships are the army and navy of the Athenians, the whole state that remains, and the great name of Athens. In this cause if any man has skill or courage greater than another, now, if ever, is the time to show it.'

After making this speech Nicias at once ordered the ships to be manned. On the other side Gylippus and the Syracu-sans saw that the Athenians were about to make their supreme effort. They had heard of their intention to use grappling-irons in the fighting and had provided against this by stretching hides over much of the upper parts of their ships, so that when the grappling-irons were thrown they would slip off again without getting a good grip. In a speech to his men Gylippus encouraged them by pointing out that they had already twice defeated the supposedly invincible Athenian navy and that now the Athenians were fighting again not with confidence but in desperation. Their skill, he said, of which they were so proud, would be of little use to them in the narrow waters and even their superior numbers would not help, since their ships would fall foul of each other. The Athenians were now aiming not so much at victory as at escape. Now, then, was the moment for the Syracusans and their allies to win freedom for themselves, to crush and destroy the most deadly enemies they had known and make this the most glorious day in the whole of their history.

After making this speech the Syracusans began to man their ships. And Nicias, half-distraught by the present position, realising how much was at stake and how imminent already the hazard, and thinking, as men do think in moments of great crisis, that when everything has been said there is still something that needs saying, again called to him personally all the captains of triremes, man by man. He addressed each of them by name, reminding them of the honours which they or their fathers had won in former years and urging them to live up to their reputations and not deface the great deeds done in the past. He reminded them of their country, the freest in the world, and of how all who lived there had liberty to live their own lives in their own way: and he said other things too—the things that men can be expected to say when they are actually on the edge of the event and do not bother to avoid using conventional language; instead they use the kind of words that are brought out on any occasion—wives, children, gods of the native land; yet still they cry out these names aloud, since, in the terror of the moment, they believe that they will help.

So, after these final appeals, which seemed to Nicias

himself still to fall short of their mark, he went back to the
shore and posted the infantry in as long a line as they could
hold by the sea, so that they might help as much as possible
in giving encouragement to the men aboard the ships. And
now Demosthenes and the other commanders put out from
their own camp and sailed straight for the barrier across the
mouth of the harbour to try and force their way out.

Part of the Syracusan fleet was stationed in front of the
entrance and the rest were all round the harbour in order to
charge the Athenians from all directions at once. In the
impetus of their first attack the Athenians overpowered the
ships stationed in front of the barrier and then tried to break
down the obstructions. But then the Syracusans and their
allies bore down on them from all sides and there was fighting not only in front of the barrier but all over the harbour.
And hard fighting it was—more so than in any of the previous
battles. Many ships crowded in upon each other in a small
area. In fact never before had so many ships fought together
in so narrow a space. There were almost two hundred of
them on the two sides. As a result there was little or no
room for manoeuvre and regular naval tactics were not
employed at all. Ship crashed into ship, and often the same
ship's company was attempting to board an enemy ship on
one side and was simultaneously being boarded on the other.
There was hand-to-hand fighting on the decks and all the
time the archers and javelin-throwers let loose a rain of
weapons from above. In the general roar of fighting and
shouting orders became impossible to hear. There was no
hanging back on either side as the Athenians fought to gain
the safety of the open sea and the Syracusans struggled to

keep the trap still closed on them.

While the issue of the battle still hung in the balance, the armies on the shore were swept by every emotion of joy and despair as they watched the fighting. For the Athenians everything depended on their navy; their fears for the future were like nothing they had ever experienced; and as the battle swung this way and that, so did their minds and feelings veer and change as they watched it from the shore. The sight was close in front of them and, as they were not all at once looking in the same direction, some saw that at one point their men were winning and took courage at the sight and cried out with joy; and others, looking at some part of the battle where their men were being defeated, cried out in lamentation and were more broken in spirit by the sight than were the men actually engaged in the fighting. Others were looking at a part of the battle where there was nothing to choose between the two sides, and, as the fighting went on and on with no decision reached, their bodies, swaying this way and that, showed the anguish and trepidation of their minds, and wretched indeed was their state, constantly on the verge of safety, constantly on the brink of destruction. One could hear sounds of all kinds coming from this one Athenian army—lamentations and cheering, cries of 'We are winning' and of 'We are losing' and all the other different exclamations bound to be made by a great army in its great danger.

Much the same were the feelings of the men on board the ships, till finally, after the battle had lasted for a long time, the Syracusans and their allies broke the Athenian resistance, followed them up with great shouting and cheering and chased them back, clearly and decisively, to the land.

And now the whole fleet, apart from the ships which were captured afloat, ran on shore, some going one way, some another, and the men fled from the ships towards the camp. As for the army on land, the period of uncertainty was over, and now one impulse overpowered them all, as they cried aloud and groaned in pain for what had happened, some going down to give help to the ships, some to guard what was left of their wall, while others (and these were now in the majority) began to think of themselves and how they could get away safe. Indeed the panic of this moment was something greater than anything they had ever known. They had lost their ships and now there seemed to be no hope of getting away safely by land, unless some miracle happened.

20. Total Destruction of the Athenian Expedition

AFTER this battle the Athenians were so overpowered by their misfortunes that they never even thought of asking for permission to take up their dead or the wreckage. Instead they wanted to retreat at once and on that very night. Demosthenes, however, went to Nicias and proposed that they should once again man the ships they had left and do their best to force their way out at dawn. He pointed out that they still had more ships fit for service than the enemy; for the Athenians had about sixty ships left and the Syracusans less than fifty. Nicias agreed with this proposal, but when they wanted to man the ships, the sailors refused to go on board. They had been so demoralised by their defeat that they no longer believed that victory was a possibility.

Hermocrates, the Syracusan general, suspected that the Athenians would retreat at once by land and wanted to march out that very day with all the land forces so as to get ahead of the Athenians and occupy the passes and build road blocks to prevent their escape. But, with the Syracusans already celebrating their victory, it was found impossible to get a force together just then. So he sent messengers to Nicias who were to pretend to be friendly to him and tell him not to start at once, as the roads over which he would have to pass were guarded. The Athenian generals believed this information was genuine and so put off the retreat by night. In fact they waited for the next day too in order to allow the soldiers to pack their essential baggage and to rest. Meanwhile Gylippus and the Syracusans set out with their field forces and posted guards at the fords of the rivers and put up fortifications at the mountain passes.

When Nicias and Demosthenes had made the best preparations they could, the time came for the army to move, two days after the naval battle. It was a terrible scene and there were many things which contributed to their dismay. They were retreating by land after having lost all their ships, and instead of their high hopes of glory and of conquest they now found themselves and the whole state of Athens in deadly peril. The dead were being left unburied and when any man recognised one of his friends among them, he was filled with grief and fear; and the living who, because they were sick or wounded, were being left behind caused more pain and were more pitiable than the dead. Their prayers and their lamentations made the rest feel impotent and helpless, as they begged to be taken with them and cried out aloud to every friend and relative whom they could see, following after them as far as they could, and, when their bodily strength failed them, still pursued them with their cries to heaven and their pitiable appeals. So the whole army was filled with tears and in such distress of mind that they found it difficult to go away even from this land of their enemies where they had already suffered so much. There was also a profound sense of shame and deep feelings of self-reproach. In fact they were like nothing so much as the fleeing population of a city that has surrendered to its besiegers, and no small city at that, since in the whole crowd of them marching together there were not less than forty thousand men. Then there was the degradation of it all, especially when they remembered the splendour and pride of their setting out and saw how mean and abject was the conclusion.

Nicias, seeing the wretched state of the army, went along the ranks and did the best he could to encourage and comfort them and, as he went from one line to another, he raised his voice louder and louder, wishing that his words should reach as many men as possible and do some good to them. 'Athenians and allies,' he said, 'even now we must still hope on. You have been saved from worse straits than these before now. And do not reproach yourselves too much for the disasters of the past or for your present sufferings. I myself am physically no stronger than any one of you (in fact, you see what my illness has done to me), nor, I think, can anyone be considered to have been luckier and more successful than I have been in my private life and in other respects; but I am now plunged into the same perils as the

meanest man here. Yet throughout my life I have worshipped
the gods as I ought, and have been just and considerate in all
my dealings with men. Because of this I still have a strong
hope for the future and these disasters do not terrify me as
they might do. Perhaps they may even come to an end, since
we have suffered enough and the gods cannot be angry with
us for ever. By now we deserve their pity rather than their
jealousy.

'And then look at yourselves: see how many first-rate
troops you have marching in your ranks, and do not be too
much alarmed. We shall hurry forward, marching by night
as well as by day, since our supplies are short, until we can
reach some friendly place among the tribes of the interior
who, because of their fear of Syracuse, will welcome us. In
a word, soldiers, you must make up your minds that to be
brave now is a matter of necessity, since no place exists close
at hand where a coward can take refuge; and that, if you
escape now, you will all see again the homes for which you
long, and the Athenians among you will build up again the
great power of Athens, fallen though it is. It is men who
make the city, and not walls or ships with no men inside
them.'

Demosthenes spoke in much the same way to the troops
under his command, and so the army moved forward in a
hollow square, Nicias leading the vanguard and Demosthenes bringing up the rear. On the first day's march they
routed a body of Syracusans and allies who were guarding
the crossing of a river and pushed on for about four miles
with the Syracusan cavalry and light troops constantly
attacking them on the flanks and from the rear. Next day

they advanced another two miles and camped on some level ground with the intention of getting food and water, since the place was inhabited. Meanwhile the Syracusans went on and fortified the pass that lay ahead of them.

All through the third and fourth days the Athenians attempted in vain to force their way over the pass. They retired by night to the plain but were now running very short of food, since the Syracusan cavalry was all around them and it was impossible to go far from the camp for supplies.

The following day too was spent in continuous fighting in the plain. Wherever the Athenians charged, the enemy would give way and then resume the attack as the Athenians retired. The attacks were being pressed from all sides, and particularly against the rearguard, and there were many killed and wounded.

During the night Nicias and Demosthenes, seeing that their route was blocked, that casualties were mounting and that the men were half-starved, decided to set out before dawn and march towards the sea in the opposite direction to the passes guarded by the Syracusans. So they lit a number of fires and marched away by night.

A night march carried out by a large army in hostile country is in any case a difficult operation; and so it happened with the Athenian army that there was much confusion. The division under Nicias, as it was leading the way, kept together and got a long distance ahead, while the troops in the rear under Demosthenes lost contact with each other and marched in some disorder. Nevertheless they reached the sea at dawn and then went forward with the intention of marching round the Syracusan position and then striking inland up one of the river valleys.

Meanwhile the Syracusans and their allies, as soon as day broke, had found that the Athenians had gone and quickly hurried after them. They caught up with Demosthenes and his troops about the time of the midday meal and attacked them at once, surrounding them with their cavalry all the more easily because they were separated from Nicias' men who were five or six miles ahead. Demosthenes found himself not only hemmed in on all sides but in a position where every advantage was on the side of the enemy. He and the Athenians were penned into a place with a wall all round it, with a road on both sides and great numbers of olive trees, and they were under a rain of missiles from every direction. Their enemies avoided coming to close quarters, knowing that in any case victory was certain. In the end terms of surrender were agreed upon. Demosthenes and his men laid down their arms and gave up what property they had on the condition that their lives should be spared. There were about six thousand of them in all who surrendered and many had been killed in the fighting which had lasted all day.

Meanwhile Nicias had marched on and, after crossing another river, had camped for the night on high ground. He knew nothing of what had happened to Demosthenes and his army and expected that they would catch up with him in the morning. But next morning the Syracusan cavalry appeared. They told him that the troops under Demosthenes had surrendered and invited him to do the same. Nicias did not believe it and a truce was arranged so that he could send a horseman to go and see. This messenger soon came back and confirmed the news of the surrender. Nicias then sent to Gylippus and offered in the name of the Athenians to pay back to Syracuse all the money she had spent on the war in return for letting his army go. This proposal was refused by Gylippus and the Syracusans, who now attacked and surrounded this army as they had the other, raining missiles on them from all sides until the evening. These men, too, were wretchedly off in their want of food and water and were suffering from wounds, from continual action and from sleeplessness.

Even so they attempted again to march away by night, but the Syracusans realised what they were doing and prevented them from getting away as they had planned.

When day came Nicias again led his army forward and the Syracusans and their allies pressed hard on them in the same way as before, showering missiles and hurling javelins in upon them from every side. The Athenians hurried on towards the river Assinarus, partly because they were under pressure from the continual attacks of cavalry, archers and slingers, and thought that things might not be so bad if they got to the river, partly because they were exhausted and were longing for water to drink. Once they reached the river, they rushed down into it, and now all discipline was at an end. Every man wanted to be the first to get across and, as the enemy persisted in his attacks, they crowded in on one another and trampled each other underfoot. Syracusan troops were stationed on the opposite bank, which was a steep one, and hurled down their weapons from above on the Athenians, most of whom, in a disordered mass, were greedily drinking in the deep river-bed. Soon the enemy came down and slaughtered them where they were. The water became foul, but still they went on drinking it, all muddy as it was and stained with blood; in fact most of them were fighting among themselves to have it.

Finally, when the dead bodies were piling up on each other in the bed of the river and the few who had got across had been cut down by the Syracusan cavalry, Nicias surrendered himself to Gylippus, whom he trusted more than he did the Syracusans, telling him and the Spartans to do what they liked with him personally, but to stop the massacre of his soldiers. After this Gylippus gave orders to take prisoners. Numbers of these were hidden by their captors and kept as slaves; in fact the whole of Sicily was full of them. The rest were taken to Syracuse and put into the stone quarries there. But large numbers of the army had been killed outright in the river, since this had been a great slaughter—greater than any that took place in this war. Very many men too had fallen in the constant attacks made on them during the march.

Later the Syracusans and their allies put both Nicias and Demosthenes to death. This was against the will of Gylippus who had wished for the glory of bringing back both the enemy generals to Sparta. One of these, Demosthenes, had been Sparta's greatest enemy, because of the campaign at Pylos, while Nicias had always been willing to make peace with Sparta whenever there was an opportunity and had been largely responsible for giving them back their men captured on the island. But Gylippus had been unable to save him. The Corinthians hated him and there were some influential Syracusans who had been secretly negotiating with him for the surrender of their city and were afraid that, if he survived, the story of these intrigues would come out. So Nicias was killed. Of all the Greeks of my time he was the one who least deserved to come to so miserable an end, since all through his life he had been good, honourable and upright.

As for the Athenian prisoners in the stone quarries, there were many of them and they were crowded together in a narrow pit where, since there was no roof over their heads, they suffered first from the heat of the sun and the closeness of the air; later came the cold autumnal nights, and the change in temperature brought on a lot of sickness. Very many died either from their wounds or from various kinds of sickness and, since there was no space, the bodies were all heaped together on top of one another, so that the smell was insupportable. At the same time they suffered from hunger and from thirst, each man receiving rations of only half a pint of water a day and a pint of corn. In fact they suffered everything which one could imagine might be suffered by men imprisoned in such a place.

So ended the events in Sicily. This was the greatest action that took place in the war and, to my mind, the greatest action that we know of in our history. To the victors it was the most brilliant of successes, and to the vanquished the most calamitous of defeats. They were utterly and entirely defeated; their sufferings were on an enormous scale; their losses were total; army, navy, everything was destroyed, and, out of many, only few returned.

Afterword

I T has seemed best to end the story told by Thucydides at this point. In fact he did write the history of the next few years, but he did not live to continue it until the end of the war. Had he been able to finish his work, we may be certain that he would have emphasised two of the points that he had made already—the amazing resilience and recuperative powers of Athens in defeat, and the relapse of the democracy into selfishness, cruelty and incompetence once they again saw any prospect of victory.

The Athenian forces in Sicily had been destroyed in 413 BC and it seemed certain to everyone except the Athenians that in the next year Sparta and her allies, now reinforced by an army and fleet from Sicily, would make an end of Athens. Soon revolt began to spread among the Athenian allies and subjects and Persia joined the war on the side of Sparta in return for a promise that after the war the Great King should regain control over the Greek cities of Asia. These cities had been freed by Athens and it is, to say the least, hard to see how Sparta, in making this treaty with Persia, could claim to be fulfilling her proclaimed role as 'liberator'.

Yet against this alliance of Sparta, Sicily and Persia, with revolt spreading in her empire and with, for a time, a state of civil war at home, Athens still held out for another nine years, till 404 BC. In fact she did more than hold her own. In the course of these years there were two occasions when Sparta, having again suffered crushing defeats at sea, offered peace on reasonable, indeed generous, terms. On each occasion the Athenian assembly refused the offer under the influence of Cleophon, a demagogue of the type of Cleon.

Much of the credit for the revival of Athenian power was due to Alcibiades, who had made himself unpopular in Sparta (partly because of a love affair with the King of Sparta's wife) and had in the end been recalled from exile and put in command. The first of the two offers of peace by Sparta was made after a victory by Alcibiades in which a fleet of sixty enemy ships was destroyed. The loss of the fleet, the army and of the Spartan commander, Mindarus, was reported to the home government by the Spartan second-in-command in the laconic dispatch: 'Ships lost. Mindarus dead. Men starving. Don't know what to do.'

By 407 BC Alcibiades was at the height of his success. Both his generalship and his diplomacy had been brilliant and he was made supreme commander of the Athenian forces. But in the restored democracy at home he still had enemies and when, in the next year, his second-in-command, at a time when Alcibiades was not present, had disobeyed his orders and risked a battle in which some twenty ships were lost, Alcibiades was deprived of his command and went into voluntary exile rather than face an Athenian court.

His fears of political intrigue and injustice were like those of Nicias and were fully justified. Soon afterwards another great naval action was fought off the coast of Asia Minor, near the Arginusae Islands. Large fleets were engaged on both sides and in the battle the Athenians lost thirteen ships sunk and twelve disabled, while the enemy lost seventy-five ships. It was after this great Athenian victory that Sparta again, and for the last time, offered peace on the basis of the *status quo* and the evacuation of Decelea.

After the victory a great storm had sprung up and the

Athenian commanders had been unable to sail to the rescue of the disabled ships, with the result that there was much loss of life among the crews. This event was followed by one of the most disgraceful and hysterical displays of injustice ever made by an Athenian assembly. Illegally and irresponsibly the six generals were tried collectively, not individually, for neglect and all were condemned and executed. Among them was the son of Pericles.

Soon after this an Athenian fleet of one hundred and eighty ships was in the Hellespont at Aegospotami. In the neighbourhood was the private castle into which Alcibiades had retired after his disgrace. From this he rode down to the shore and advised the Athenian commanders to move their fleet from what he considered a dangerous and exposed position. They told him to mind his own business. Next day the Spartan admiral, Lysander, surprised the Athenians before they had time to man their ships and destroyed the whole fleet. Only nine out of one hundred and eighty ships got away.

This was the end. While Athens herself was impregnable, it was impossible to bring food into the city and impossible to hold out against starvation. Athens was forced to accept the terms dictated by Sparta, which were more generous than many of Sparta's allies, notably the Thebans, liked. These allies were in favour of killing all the adult males and of enslaving the women and children, as Athens had done in the case of Melos.

What Athens had to agree to was this: the surrender of all her fleet except for twelve ships, Spartan control over her foreign policy, the giving up of her empire and the demoli-

tion of her Long Walls and of the fortifications of Piraeus—
all the political and military structure that had been begun
by Themistocles and extended by Pericles. In April 404 BC
Lysander and his fleet sailed into Piraeus—and the Spartans
and their allies, to the music of flutes, began the work of
demolishing the Long Walls. According to the account of
Xenophon, it was in the belief that 'this day was the beginning of freedom in Greece'.

It was, of course, nothing of the sort. Indeed it would be
truer to say that this occasion marked the beginning of the
end of that peculiar form of freedom enjoyed by the Greek
city-state. The day was coming for the great impersonal
empires, first of Alexander and his successors and then of
Rome. Nothing like the complete, total and confident democracy of Pericles has ever existed again.

Thucydides quite clearly felt the spell of the ideal of
Pericles and equally clearly he saw the injustices, the cruel-
ties, the selfishness and the stupidity of the same democracy
under the stress of war and under divided and incompetent
leadership. We may regret that he did not live to complete
the story of the war and its aftermath and may be certain
that he would have done it much more forcibly and brilliantly than Xenophon or anyone else could do it. But one
regrets even more that he could not have lived still longer,
indeed up to the present day. He would then have seen
something which even he, perhaps, never imagined. Pericles
had declared that Athens was an education to Greece. She
remained so, and in the century after the war laid the
foundations and created the models for our philosophy,
science and criticism, just as, in Pericles' own day, she had

done for politics, art, drama, history and architecture. Since then she has been an education, not only for Greece, but for a world far bigger than that of which Pericles could have dreamed. Thucydides would have rejoiced to see how strictly true were Pericles' words: 'Hatred does not last for long, but the brilliance of the present is the glory of the future, stored up for ever in the memory of man.'

REX WARNER

University of Connecticut, 1969

TITLES IN THE NEW WINDMILL SERIES

Bessie Head: *When Rain Clouds Gather*
John Hersey: *A Single Pebble*
Georgette Heyer: *Regency Buck*
Alfred Hitchcock: *Sinister Spies*
Geoffrey Household: *Rogue Male; A Rough Shoot; Prisoner of the Indies*
Fred Hoyle: *The Black Cloud*
Irene Hunt: *Across Five Aprils*
Henry James: *Washington Square*
Josephine Kamm: *Young Mother; Out of Step; Where Do We Go From Here?*
John Knowles: *A Separate Peace*
D. H. Lawrence: *Sea and Sardinia*; *The Fox* and *The Virgin and the Gipsy; Selected Tales*
Marghanita Laski: *Little Boy Lost*
Harper Lee: *To Kill a Mockingbird*
Laurie Lee: *As I Walked Out One Mid-Summer Morning*
Ursula Le Guin: *A Wizard of Earthsea*
Doris Lessing: *The Grass is Singing*
C. Day Lewis: *The Otterbury Incident*
Lorna Lewis: *Leonardo the Inventor*
Martin Lindsay: *The Epic of Captain Scott*
Kathleen Lines: *The House of the Nightmare*
Jack London: *The Call of the Wild; White Fang*
Carson McCullers: *The Member of the Wedding*
Lee McGiffen: *On the Trail to Sacramento*
Wolf Mankowitz: *A Kid for Two Farthings*
Olivia Manning: *The Play Room*
James Vance Marshall: *A River Ran Out of Eden*
John Masefield: *Sard Harker; The Bird of Dawning; The Midnight Folk; The Box of Delights*
W. Somerset Maugham: *The Kite and Other Stories*
Guy de Maupassant: *Prisoner of War and Other Stories*
Laurence Meynell: *Builder and Dreamer*
Yvonne Mitchell: *Cathy Away*
Honoré Morrow: *The Splendid Journey*
Bill Naughton: *The Goalkeeper's Revenge*
E. Nesbit: *The Railway Children; The Story of the Treasure Seekers*
Wilfrid Noyce: *South Col*
Scott O'Dell: *Island of the Blue Dolphins*
George Orwell: *Animal Farm*
Merja Otava: *Priska*
John Prebble: *The Buffalo Soldiers*
J. B. Priestley: *Saturn Over the Water*
Lobsang Rampa: *The Third Eye*
Arthur Ransome: *Swallows and Amazons*